Little Hearts Books

The Gentle Parent
Positive, Practical, Effective Discipline

International best-selling, award-winning author, L.R.Knost, is an independent child development researcher and founder and director of the advocacy and consulting group, Little Hearts/Gentle Parenting Resources, as well as a monthly contributor to *The Natural Parent Magazine*. She is also a babywearing, breastfeeding, co-sleeping, homeschooling mother of six. Her children are a twenty-six-year-old married father of two; a twenty-four-year-old married Family Therapist; a nineteen-year-old university pre-med student; fifteen- and eight-year-old sweet, funny, socially active, homeschooled girls; and an adorable and active toddler. Other works by L.R.Knost include *Two Thousand Kisses a Day: Gentle Parenting Through the Ages and Stages; Whispers Through Time: Communication-Based Parenting;* and *Jesus, The Gentle Parent: Gentle Christian Parenting;* as well as her children's picture books, *A Walk in the Clouds,* the soon-to-be-released *Grumpykins* series, and *Petey's Listening Ears*, the first in the *Wisdom for Little Hearts* series, which are humorous and engaging tools for parents, teachers, and caregivers to use in implementing gentle parenting techniques in their homes and schools.

*Note: Information contained in this book is for educational purposes only and should not be construed as medical or mental health counsel.

The Gentle Parent
Positive, Practical, Effective Discipline

L.R.Knost

A Little Hearts Handbook
Little Hearts Books, LLC. ▪ U.S.A.

Photography credit: Melissa Lynsay Photography

I'm here to parent you, my child
When you're calm and when you're wild

To hear, to share, to lead, to guide
Hand-in-hand and side-by-side

Together we will learn and grow
Play and talk and come and go

When times are hard and moods are grey
You and I will find our way

I'll be right here to see you through
Guide, support, and listen, too

I'll teach. I'll learn. I'll help. I'll hold.
So you will know as years unfold

That nothing you can say or do
Will make my love grow less for you

L.R.Knost

Table of Contents

Middle Childhood: Becoming Their Own Person

Gentle Parenting: Teens and Beyond

Appendix A

Appendix B

Appendix C

~ Introduction ~

Chapter 1

The Problem with Punishment
[From *Two Thousand Kisses a Day:*
Gentle Parenting Through the Ages and Stages]

Want to know a dirty little secret about punishment?

It doesn't work.

Punishment may be able to control a child's behavior temporarily while they're small or when they are in their parents' presence, but it cannot control the person. As with all humans, outward behavior is merely a reflection of our inner selves: our needs, our hurts, our emotional states.

While the temporary 'payoff' of punishment may be compliance, the need behind the behavior is never addressed and those needs merely get driven underground and often emerge later in more potentially damaging behaviors such as lying, sneaking, anger, outright rebellion, depression, aggression, addictions, etc.

In the same way that treating a brain tumor by merely taking a pain reliever doesn't address the underlying issue, masking the symptoms of an underlying need with punishment-induced compliance doesn't solve the problem; it intensifies it.

Want to know another dirty little secret about punishment?

It requires constant escalation.

In order to maintain the temporary effect of controlling behavior, the punishment, or threats of punishment, must constantly be ramped up. Parents who start out with popping a tiny hand escalate to smacking a chubby little leg, then paddling a small bottom. Over time, as their children's needs which have been driven underground emerge in ever-increasing behavioral issues, parents often find that they are resorting to yelling and threats and physical punishment more and more often.

Even parents who use punishment-based parenting approaches other than physical punishment find that they must escalate and escalate to keep their children under 'control.' Behavior charts, time-outs, grounding, and removing privileges are some examples of non-physical punishment-based parenting. While these behavior modification techniques may be less painful to children physically, they still don't address the underlying needs being communicated by the behavior and often are nearly as destructive to the parent/child relationship.

Using isolation such as time-outs or sending children to their room separates them from their source of guidance and comfort just when they need it the most and not only misses a golden opportunity to help the child learn coping mechanisms for dealing with their emotions, but also fractures the very connection that should provide the safety for expressing those emotions. Using behavior charts, removal of privileges, grounding, etc. separates children from their parents by creating an 'us-against-them' mentality that inevitably leads to conflict instead of creating a teamwork mentality that leads to cooperation.

Here's the thing, effective parenting and, more specifically, effective discipline, don't require punishment. Equating discipline with punishment is an unfortunate, but common misconception. The root word in discipline is actually *disciple* which in the verb form means to guide, lead, teach, model, and encourage. In the noun form *disciple* means one who embraces the teaching of, follows the example of, and models their life after.

On the flip side, the root word in punishment is the Latin word *punire* which in verb form means to penalize, chastise, castigate, inflict harm, humiliate. There is no noun form of *punire* or its English equivalent, punishment.

Many of today's most popular self-proclaimed parenting 'experts' equate physical punishment with discipline and go to great lengths to describe the best methods and tools for hitting children as well as instructing parents to maintain a calm, controlled, and even cheerful demeanor as they 'lovingly' hit their children.

It is interesting to note here that, when it comes to the law, crimes of passion are treated as less heinous than premeditated, planned, and purposefully executed crimes which are termed 'in cold blood.' And yet when physically punishing a child, a crime in many places across the globe, hitting in anger or frustration (i.e. passion) is deemed wrong by proponents of spanking, while hitting children with calm and deliberate intent (i.e. premeditation) is encouraged.

It is also interesting to note that, in the not-too-distant past, husbands hitting their wives was also viewed as not only a societal norm, but also a necessary part of maintaining a harmonious, successful marriage. In fact, a man who epitomizes the words calm and controlled, Sean Connery, shared his thoughts on the 'reasonable smacking' of his wife in a 1987 interview with Barbara Walters in which he explained the necessity of using punitive methods to control women.

The core belief behind 'reasonable smacking' of wives was that there was no other effective way to control them. I agree. If controlling another human being is the goal, then force is necessary. Fear, intimidation, threats, power-plays, physical pain, those are the means of control.

But, if growing healthy humans is the goal, then building trust relationships, encouraging, guiding, leading, teaching, and communicating are the tools for success.

Many parents simply don't know what else to do. They were raised with spanking and other punishment-based parenting methods as a means of control and "turned out okay" so they default to their own parents' choices without researching alternatives to spanking or considering whether "okay" could be improved upon.

Consider this, more than ninety-percent of American parents admit to spanking their children, and yet the common contention is that it's a decline in spanking that is responsible for the purportedly escalating rates of youth violence and crime. Is it really the less than ten-percent of children who aren't spanked who are responsible for all the problems of our society? Or could it be that the ninety-percent of children who are subject to violence at home in the form of being slapped, paddled, smacked, yanked, whipped, popped, spanked, etc. are taking those lessons out into the world? Is it just possible that children who are hit learn to hit? That children who are hurt learn to hurt? Perhaps the lesson they are learning is that 'might is right' and violence is the answer to their problems, the outlet for their stress, the route to getting others to do what they want.

People throughout history have complained about 'the trouble with kids today' and they've pinned all the ills of their society on supposedly permissive parenting. They've ranted about out-of-control children, disrespectful youth, entitlement, spoiling, disobedience, violence, self-centeredness, etc:

> *"The children now love luxury. They have bad manners, contempt for authority, they show disrespect to their elders.... They no longer rise when elders enter the room. They contradict their parents, chatter before company, gobble up dainties at the table, cross their legs, and are tyrants over their teachers."* ~Socrates, 5th Century BC

> *"What is happening to our young people? They disrespect their elders, they disobey their parents. They ignore the law. They riot in the streets inflamed with wild notions. Their morals are decaying. What is to become of them?"* ~Plato, 5th Century BC

> *"I see no hope for the future of our people if they are dependent on frivolous youth of today, for certainly all youth are reckless beyond words... When I was young, we were taught to be discreet and respectful of elders, but the present youth are exceedingly wise [disrespectful] and impatient of restraint"* ~Hesiod, 8th Century BC

"The world is passing through troublous times. The young people of today think of nothing but themselves. They have no reverence for parents or old age. They are impatient of all restraint. They talk as if they knew everything, and what passes for wisdom with us is foolishness with them. As for the girls, they are forward, immodest and unladylike in speech, behavior and dress." ~Peter the Hermit, 13th Century AD

Sounds familiar, doesn't it? Maybe, though, there isn't really any 'trouble with kids today.' Maybe the problem is with parents who repeat the patterns their own parents set or with societies who view normal stages of development as somehow abnormal.

Maybe 'kids today' are just kids like they have been through the ages, full of exuberance and curiosity and learning their way in a great big world, and a listening ear, gentle guidance, and trusted arms to turn to when inevitable mistakes are made are really all children need to grow up into kind, helpful, responsible, productive members of our society.

The bottom line is that addressing our children's underlying needs, the actual causes of their behavior instead of just the behavior itself, is a far more effective parental approach as well as being significantly better for a healthy, mutually respectful parent/child relationship.

Let's send our children out into the world as adults with their needs met, with coping mechanisms in place for those times when the stresses overwhelm them, and with the knowledge of a safe haven where comfort is always available when the world hurts them. Let's learn how to seek solutions with our children instead of inflicting retributions on our children. And let's start sowing peace instead of violence in our homes and in the hearts of our children to make a better tomorrow for all of us.

~ A Gentle Beginning ~

Chapter 2

Foundations: Setting the Stage for Discipline

I'm sorry for the sleepless nights
The times I make you sigh
I'm sorry for the crankiness
The times I scream and cry
I'm sorry I don't have the words
For why I need you so
But I can tell you this one thing
That I need you to know
You are the center of my world
You're everything to me
You are my sun, my moon, my stars
You're all that I can see
I'm only little a short time
Soon I won't need you so
But I will love you all my life
Just wanted you to know

~Your Baby

Your sweet new baby has just arrived in this great big, beautiful world. As you cuddle and rock and sing lullabies and kiss tiny fingers and toes and memorize every adorable feature on your little one's face, did you know that you are setting the stage for later discipline? Crazy, huh? The fact is, though, that every interaction you have with your children from the moment they are born molds your relationship with them, and with gentle parenting, it is the trust relationship you are building now that everything else will be built upon.

Laying the trust foundation for gentle discipline may seem like a lofty goal to an exhausted parent of a new little one, but the thing is that it isn't an added burden to your already overburdened life. It is in the ordinary moments of life itself that you are building your relationship with your child, and it is in those moments that you decide whether your relationship will be built on control and correction or built on trust and connection. The difference between a punitive parent and a gentle parent is not about how much a child is loved. The difference is found in the parents' view of parenting.

The parent who views parenting as an adult-controlled relationship tends to seek to establish their dominance from the moment their baby arrives, making sure that their little one adapts to the existing family dynamic and submits to parental authority. This parent will often set up a rigid schedule that fits their lifestyle and then train their baby to fit into that plan by such means as sleep training and scheduled feedings. The type of discipline these parenting choices set the stage for is one of external controls, power struggles, and punitive corrections in a parent-centric family dynamic.

The parent who views parenting as an interactive, trust-based relationship will focus on creating a responsive atmosphere from the moment their baby arrives, making sure that their little one knows that they are safe, that they are heard, and that their needs will be met. This parent responds to their baby's cries quickly and consistently, day and night, and seeks to establish a family rhythm that meets everyone's needs. The type of discipline these parenting choices set the stage for is one of interaction, cooperation, and guidance in a family-centric dynamic.

Understanding that your parenting choices in infancy affect the style of discipline you will want to follow with your child later on is helpful because it inspires an awareness in you that you are growing a person, not just taking care of a baby. Knowing that meeting your baby's needs quickly and consistently isn't just about their momentary comfort, as important as that is, but also about your long-term relationship will help you to remain focused and committed when your parenting choices are challenged by mainstream parents who tell you that you are going to spoil your baby or by well-meaning relatives who tell you that training your baby is the only way to raise them properly.

The fact is that you can't spoil a baby. Period. Think about it this way—food spoils when it is ignored, mishandled, and neglected. That rotten potato stinking up the pantry didn't get that way because it was well taken care of, but because it was ignored until it went bad. That wilted lettuce in the back of the refrigerator didn't get that way because it was wrapped well, but because it wasn't handled properly. That moldy orange languishing in the produce bin didn't get that way because it was handled with care, but because it was neglected and forgotten.

By the same token, children aren't spoiled when their needs are taken care of promptly with gentleness and respect. In fact, since the word spoiled is defined as "devalued, damaged, and impaired" the case could be made that children are spoiled when their needs are ignored, mishandled, and neglected.

In gentle discipline, the focus is on growing an ability and desire within our children to regulate their own emotions and behavior. The ability comes with time, maturity, guidance, and consistent modeling on our part. The desire comes from the atmosphere of cooperation, understanding, and trust that you are building day by day, night by night, gentle response by gentle response.

If you've started off your parenting with an adult-controlled relationship and want to know if you can change to the trust-based relationship foundational to gentle discipline, the answer is yes. It will take patience, commitment, healing, and rebuilding of your relationship to make such a fundamental shift, but it can most definitely be done. (See Chapter Twenty-Three for some ideas about how to begin.)

The thing is, parents, trust takes time. You can build it from the beginning, or you can repair it later, but it is most certainly easier to build a healthy relationship than to repair a broken one. Your choices *matter*, and they matter right from the start. Making gentle choices from the beginning ensures that you have a secure foundation to build upon.

Chapter 3

Castles in the Air: Building on Trust

"Castles in the air are the stuff of daydreams, it's true, but they can be dreams come true if you take the time to build them."

Imagine you are building a castle, as lovely inside as it is out. In addition to wanting to build a strong, resilient fortress that will stand the test of time, you want your castle to be open, warm, and inviting. You want it to not only reflect its builder's hopes and dreams, but also to have its own unique character, unlike anything that has ever been seen before or will ever be seen again. Will your castle be a haven for the weary and disheartened? Will it be a shining light in a dark world? Will it guard the helpless or guide the lost? Will it enthrall the world with its artistic flair or calm the world with its serene wisdom? There's no way to know everything that your castle will offer the world or will have to withstand through the years, but you do know that laying a secure foundation and building stable walls and filling your castle with beauty and light will provide everything your castle needs, no matter what the future holds.

Through the ages, master carpenters, painters, craftsmen, and the like went through grueling apprenticeships so that the last vestiges of immaturity and self-focus and rashness left over from their youth were chiseled away, enabling them to create the spectacular structures and stunning works of art that we call masterpieces today.

Parenting in infancy can be much like that grueling apprenticeship as you are transformed through the sleepless nights and aching arms and soiled clothes from a mere person into a gentle parent. As your new little one grows and you continue to build and reinforce your trust relationship, you will begin to get to know the unique individual that you have the privilege of growing and guiding into adulthood.

Building is hard work, though, whether you're building a castle or a relationship, and it can seem like a thankless, endless task when the relationship you are building is with a tiny human who can't talk, needs you night and day, and the only return on your time and effort is a constant stream of spit-up and poop punctuated by the occasional adorably toothless grin.

This is where the discipline of sacrifice begins to mature and shape you as a parent so that you can grow and guide your child. It is a crucible which will refine and define you as a human to prepare you for the work of building a healthy human. Here is where you will grow in the skills you want to pass along to your child—patience, kindness, generosity, endurance, self-control, compassion.

This time requires a letting go of self, an embracing of a new life-stage in which another's needs supersede yours, possibly for the first time ever. It is exhausting, challenging, stretching, confusing, exasperating, and downright terrifying at times, but it is in the sacrifices you make that you will find your strength and purpose.

And it is this discipline of sacrifice that will hone your ability to control your own emotions and kneejerk reactions when you are tested in your parenting, and help you to stand firm when you are challenged for your parenting decisions, and see you through the dark hours when you doubt your ability to be the parent you want to be.

These early years of your parenting journey may seem to stretch on forever, but the time will come that you will discover just how fleeting they really were. The sacrifices you make now in sleep and comfort and convenience may feel overwhelming, but as the years pass by, the parent you become will thank you for your gift of growth and strength and purpose. You may not be able to imagine now, in these early stages of life when your baby is so new and small, that one day they will be an adult just like you, but that is exactly what they will be…an adult *just like you*. So as you begin to grow your own little masterpiece, your dream come true, taking this time to become the adult you want your child to be is like drafting the blueprint for your castle and setting its cornerstone securely into place.

Chapter 4

Safe Surroundings

If growing our children is like building a castle, then setting boundaries is like digging a moat around the castle. In the earliest stages of childhood, one form of setting boundaries is removing temptations, putting up baby gates, installing cabinet locks, etc. These physical limitations, otherwise known as baby-proofing, are an effective and gentle beginning to the process of boundary setting. A common misconception is that removing temptations is passive, indulgent, or lazy parenting, but it is actually proactive parenting, whereas passive, indulgent, lazy parenting would be to simply set no limits at all. Baby-proofing is not only for a little one's safety, but it is also a visual form of limit-setting which is easily understandable for little ones and easy for parents to maintain.

Limit-setting at this stage also takes the form of such things as gently holding little hands out of the way during messy diaper changes, consistently keeping a small child happily occupied in a highchair or lap while in a restaurant, babywearing or using a cart or stroller in stores, gently removing a tiny biter from the breast before they can chomp down, and carefully disentangling little fingers from a fistful of hair.

Parents often have the misconception that setting boundaries occurs when a child misbehaves, but the fact is that the word 'misbehave' is misused. Children don't 'mis'behave. They behave, either positively or negatively, to communicate. Small children communicate through their behavior because that is the only method of communication they have. Even when they become verbal, though, they still aren't able to articulate big feelings and subtle problems well verbally, so as parents it's our role to 'listen between the lines' of our children's behavior to discern the need being communicated. Setting boundaries is not about 'mis'behavior. It's about guiding behavior, and guidance is something we provide through everyday interactions with our children.

Repetition is the hallmark of the early years of parenting, from the endless tasks of diapering and feeding to the endless explorations of a curious toddler. There is no way, and no point in trying, to make a child stop acting like a child. There are, though, gentle ways to guide a child through the normal developmental stages safely and peacefully. The repetitious nature of boundary-setting in the early years is a bit like washing your hair, "Lather, rinse, repeat, repeat, repeat, repeat…" Knowing that and accepting it makes the seemingly endless repetitions, reminders, and redirections a bit easier to handle.

As your little one becomes mobile, you will find that setting boundaries is an ongoing, moment-by-moment interaction with your child.

- When your little explorer decides that the power outlets must be plumbed for their secrets, you will need to redirect their attention, often again and again, and take safety measures such as installing outlet covers.

- When your intrepid climber challenges the laws of gravity by scaling furniture, counters, stairs, and anything and everything else that cries out to be conquered, you will need to remove, remind, and redirect them again and again along with using baby gates and other measures to ensure their safety.

- When your curious little scientist investigates the contents of your kitchen cabinets looking for ingredients to gleefully mix and mash, you will need to rescue your 'ingredients' and your child, offer alternative, safer ingredients to investigate, and install some cabinet locks.

The thing to remember is that parenting isn't about fixing a problem. It's about growing a person, and people have their own thoughts and opinions and ideas and plans, even when they are tiny people. Working with our children instead of against them creates a cooperative, teamwork dynamic as opposed to an adversarial, us-against-them atmosphere ripe for conflict.

Childhood should be a safe and lovely place to grow and explore and imagine, a place filled with possibilities, a place where it's okay to hope and dream and try and fail and try again...kind of like a castle in the air.

People always say, "Choose your battles," in parenting. Let's choose peace, instead. After all, our children aren't our enemies, and childhood shouldn't be a battleground.

Chapter 5

Reasonable Expectations

It has been said that expectations are the cause of conflict, and there is great truth to that. Expecting a forecasted sunny day but getting drenched in the rain, expecting a Christmas bonus but going home for the holidays with a fruit basket, expecting a romantic dinner for two but ending up serving wings and nachos to a houseful of football fanatics, all of these experiences are potential sources of stress and conflict in our lives, our interactions, our relationships.

And parenting is no less vulnerable to the stress and conflict caused by expectations, particularly when it comes to the often unreasonable expectations we have of these tiny humans we are growing and guiding and upon whom we hang so many of our hopes and dreams. Since the heart of gentle parenting is to work with our children in developmentally appropriate ways, it makes sense to take a moment and examine our expectations to make sure that they are, in fact, age-appropriate developmental expectations. In keeping with the castle theme from the last few chapters, we can call this a tour of our little castles in the air…

Our first stop on the tour is the sleeping chamber. It is here that many new parents meet their first conflict in parenting when their expectations run headlong into reality. When exhausted parents say they feel like they've been run over by a truck, maybe what they mean is that they're reeling from the impact of hitting that brick wall of reality at three o'clock in the morning!

> *Here's the expectation*: Many parents believe (often because they've been told by well-meaning friends and relatives) that infants should 'sleep like a baby,' meaning that after the first few weeks of life they should be able to sleep for six or eight or even ten hours

at a stretch, and if they don't, then there is a problem that needs to be fixed.

Here's the reality: "Infants and toddlers are natural night-wakers which has been shown to be protective against SIDS (Sudden Infant Death Syndrome). Children tend to differ not in whether they wake in the night or not, but in whether they need help being soothed back to sleep or not based on their own unique personality, health, environmental factors, etc. Sleeping patterns are neither a sign of a 'good' baby or a 'bad' baby, just a normal baby. Even adults tend to wake frequently at night, but typically just roll over or adjust their blankets or take a quick trip to the bathroom and then go back to sleep. They just often don't remember any of it in the morning! In reality, night-waking is simply a biological norm[1] that has been misconstrued as 'problems sleeping' or 'sleep issues' by the demands of our modern, hectic lifestyle." (From *Two Thousand Kisses a Day*)

Here's the solution: Shift your expectations to align with the reality that night-waking is normal and that, in time, your little one will grow out of their need for you to help soothe them back to sleep. Shifting your perspective will help you to stop stressing about your child's natural sleep patterns and work with them to find ways to get the sleep you both need and even to get some other things done, as well, whether it's by napping while your little one naps or cosleeping[2] or babywearing.

Our next stop on the tour is the castle kitchen where you will find a very limited variety of foods consisting mainly of crackers, bananas, and cheese. It is here that many believe the first food fight originated as unknowing parents tried to feed their little taste-tester a few bites of foie gras, only to find it suddenly splattered against their own shocked faces.

Here's the expectation: Many parents believe that enforcing a one-bite-rule or even demanding that a child eat whatever is placed in front of them is necessary to raise a healthy eater.

Here's the reality: Healthy eaters are products of mature taste buds, not force-feeding. Infants don't need anything other than breastmilk for the first year, and after that breastmilk still provides most of the nutrients small children need throughout the toddler years[3] if you choose to continue nursing for the two-plus years recommended by the World Health Organization.[4] Even if you are not nursing your toddler, though, they are still very small and don't have vast nutritional needs. In fact, their tiny tummies are no bigger than the size of their tiny fists![5]

Here's the solution: Simply offer a variety of healthy foods throughout the day, limit sweets to occasional treats, provide plenty of outdoor time to build up a healthy appetite, and let your child decide when they are hungry and how much they want to eat. Involving your little one in the planning, shopping for, and preparing of meals is also a great way to get them interested in a variety of foods. And if a day or two goes by with nothing passing those sweet little lips other than cheese, cheese, and more cheese, don't sweat it. At least you know they're laying in a good supply of calcium for when they switch their allegiance to bananas!

Our final stop on the tour of great expectations is the hall of temptations. It is here, more often than not, that most conflicts arise in the early years of parenting, because it is here that parents first discover the truth that their adorable little person is, in fact, human.

Here's the expectation: Parents are often of the opinion that a simple 'no' should suffice to let their little one know that some things are off limits. Shouldn't a child just trust that their parents know everything and be content with that? After all, parents are adults, and adults know how stuff works and what stuff is dangerous and what stuff might pinch a little finger and what stuff feels hot and what stuff tastes like, right?

Here's the reality: Toddlers don't care whether you know stuff or not. They want to know stuff! And they get to know stuff through touching and climbing and tasting and pushing and pulling and ripping and throwing and picking up and putting down stuff. A twelve-month-old who repeatedly pulls the cat's tail may be experimenting with the interesting sound the cat makes, the soft texture of the fur, her own feeling of power, or just trying to find out if pulling the tail is as 'not-okay' after her nap as it was before. Little ones too young to grasp the concept of permanence cannot be expected to understand the permanent nature of rules and limits. But even beyond that, young children have little to no impulse control, meaning they live very much in the moment, because the executive function portion of their brain which controls forethought is still in the very early stages of development.[6]

Here's the solution: Start with an understanding of age-appropriate behaviors such as an insatiable curiosity and drive to explore. Operating from a place of understanding will help you to empathize with your toddler's need to discover all there is to know in this great big, wonderful world so that you can set reasonable boundaries while providing plenty of opportunities to taste and try and touch and test and tinker while still keeping your little knowledge-seeker safe and secure.

Chapter 6

The Three C's of Gentle Discipline

Our final installment in the castle theme is a visit to the Tower Keep. It is in the Keep that parents gather the implements of parenting in preparation for guiding their children through the ups and downs and ins and outs of childhood.

Many parents, still unknowingly hurting from their own upbringing, stock up on ammunition and supplies as if preparing for a siege in a long, bloody battle. They shore up their defenses, consult with other battle-worn parents, commiserate with wounded mothers, and collaborate with tough-love fathers so that they will be ready for the dreaded battles ahead.

But here's the thing, human nature dictates that if you have a weapon and believe you have the right or the need to use it, you will use it. If you build an arsenal against your children to try to control them, you will use it, and you will both be damaged. You will both suffer. Your trust-relationship will be broken, and the adult you raise will be hurt as much as you are hurt.

Gentle parents, however, gather resources to guide their children through childhood instead of preparing to battle their children for control of their childhood. In gentle parenting, it is here in the Keep, the core of the castle where the family lives and loves and works and plays together, that you find the heart of gentle parenting, the bedrocks of gentle discipline ~ Connection, Communication, and Cooperation. These three elements, when interwoven with threads of understanding, respect, and love, are what combine to create the beautiful tapestry of a peaceful, happy home.

With the goal of equipping their children with internal controls rather than trying to control them with external forces, the gentle parent gathers the tools of…

…Connection such as physical affection, empathy, imaginative play, and shared interests;

…and the tools of Communication which are listening, reflecting, validating, sharing, and discussing;

…and, finally, the tools of Cooperation such as inviting, encouraging, supporting, and interacting.

These resources, each falling under the heading of one of the Three C's of gentle discipline, are designed to work together in a harmonic rhythm like the syncopation of a loom's up and down motion, strengths balancing weaknesses, highs interwoven with lows, quick beats knotting and slow beats untangling, all together creating a tapestry of the beautiful order and joyful chaos of a gentle childhood.

~ Toddler Time ~

Chapter 7

Sandbox Soapbox: Toddler Insights

As we step into the toddler zone, let's start where we should always start…with observing and understanding so that we can not only grow happy, well-rounded children, but also grow as parents and as humans ourselves. So to begin to implement the Three C's of gentle discipline—Connection, Communication, and Cooperation—let's take a peek inside the mind of the toddler by listening in on a sandbox conversation at the park:

Toddler 1: *You look a little frazzled, Dude. Hard day?*

Toddler 2: *Hard doesn't even begin to describe my day! I love my mommy to pieces, but seriously, she does NOT know how to share. I took one little thing out of her purse, and she freaked! Snatching and saying, "Mine!" and everything. And right in the middle of the store, too! So embarrassing. Everybody was looking at me, rolling their eyes. I felt like a total failure.*

Toddler 1: *I hear you! I have the same problem. And mine has been getting into EVERYTHING, too! Like, I stashed my cracker under the couch so I could have a little snack later, and she totally threw it in the trash! Who does that?*

Toddler 2: *You think that's bad? Check this. I'm minding my own business, just chillin' with my toys, and she just snatches me up and carts me off and straps me in the highchair, no warning at all. And I'm not even hungry! Then she gets all upset when I do a little physics with my food. Btw, so cool how sometimes it falls straight down and sometimes it splats against the wall. I think it has something to do with the consistency of the food and the angle of my trajectory. Just a working theory atm, though.*

Toddler 1: *Cool! Let me know what you figure out. How about this. I can't get* anything *done! No joke! I spent all morning building this stellar block tower. Dude, you should have seen this thing. It was epic! So, I walk away for like one second, and she dumps the whole thing in the toy box! An entire morning's work, gone. I don't know why I bother sometimes.*

Toddler 2: *Same! And what's with this new 'time-out' thing mine's into all of a sudden? I get the slightest bit upset about something, and, just when I need a cuddle, she sticks me in this chair and* won't *let me get up! Like a chair is a good hugger? Really?*

Toddler 1: *That is just wrong. Hey, how about this whole potty training dealio? She wants me to do my business in a little plastic* bowl*. We eat out of those things! Seriously, you gotta wonder what goes on in their brains sometimes.*

Toddler 2: *You're lucky. Mine keeps propping me up on that big white contraption with water in it. I could* drown*! And you should see what happens when she pushes down that handle in the back. Can you say vortex of DOOM?!?*

Toddler 1: *Not cool, Dude, not cool at all! Are you dealing with tantrums yet? Mine has got a temper like you wouldn't believe! Anytime she doesn't get her way, watch out for the fireworks! She yells and flaps her arms and stomps around, and, I hate to say it, but she's starting to hit. Like that's going to solve anything. I have no idea how to handle these aggression issues! Why can't they just be reasonable like us?*

Toddler 2: *I think it's a communication issue, myself. I mean, they're just barely starting to understand us when we talk to them, so I try to cut mine a little slack when she starts getting frustrated. I just stay close, maybe pat her arm or offer her a toy. Sometimes she settles down a bit and starts smiling again, but sometimes she just needs a little time to calm down. I stay present, though, so she knows I'm always there for her.*

Toddler 1: *I think you're messing up there, Dude. You need to walk away, just walk away and let her deal. If you comfort her, she'll expect you to help her process her emotions, and that'll lead to dependency issues, mark my words! When she freaks, you've got to* force *her to control herself! When she's ready to be reasonable and listen, then you can be friends again.*

Toddler 2: *I don't know. Mine flat out won't listen. I can't tell you how many times I have to ask her to play with me before she finally looks up from her toy. What is it with parents and electronics, anyway? And then all she does is say, "Just a minute, hon." What exactly is a minute, btw?*

Toddler 1: *'Just a minute' means 'This is more important than you,' Dude. Come on, get with the program. You have to* make *them pay attention! Yell. Throw something. Bite the cat. Whatever it takes! Don't let them get away with disrespecting you like that or they'll never pay attention.*

Toddler 2: *Word. Talk about getting with the program, how do you handle the sleep issues? I just cannot* take *another sleepless night! She keeps me up for hours every. single. night. It starts out great, bath-time, a book and cuddles, but then she just clocks out like I'm some kind of a toy she can switch off when it gets dark! And, man, is it dark. I don't know what's living in my closet, but it is ginormous!*

Toddler 1: *Sleep training, Dude! It's the* only *way.*
They turn that light out and shut the door, you follow
them! Every. Time. *Or, if you're too scared (totally get*
that, btw) then just start hollering and don't stop. If you
can't sleep, make sure they can't, either! And don't give
in. Not even once. You let them get away with that stuff
one time, and you'll never get any sleep, ever! They
have to learn that it's their job to take care of you day
and *night, even if all you need is a hug!*

Toddler 2: *Got it. Oh, man, here she comes. Seriously,*
do you have this problem, too? We're at the park.
Everybody's having a good time. And she just up and
decides to leave. I think she's got some anti-social
tendencies. I'm thinking of having her tested.

Toddler 1: *Same here! But I'm working on it. They've*
got to learn it's not all about them, and it's our job to
teach them. Look, here comes mine, too. Watch and
learn, Dude. I'm using the arched-back, flail and wail
today. Deep breath and, "No! No! Noooooo…"

Seeing our own actions from another perspective is
uncomfortable, no doubt, but the understanding we can achieve
is well worth the discomfort if we can learn and grow from it as
parents. As Maya Angelou, American author, poet, and self-
described Renaissance Woman, wrote, "Do the best you can
until you know better. Then when you know better, do better."

Chapter 8

Toddlers, Tantrums, and Time-in's, Oh my!

When a little person feels frustrated, overwhelmed, or just plain old out-of-sorts (read: tantrum time!) it's tempting for parents to focus on correction rather than connection. But when children are intensely stressed, the prefrontal cortex of the brain, which in early childhood is an underdeveloped, mushy grey sponge waiting to be formed, is flooded with cortisol, the 'stress hormone.' The result is what is known as the fight-freeze-or-flight syndrome in which higher brain functions (learning, reason, self-control) are markedly hampered and lower brain functions (instinct, physical reactions) take over. This is an in-built survival mechanism that gradually comes under conscious control through years of growth in a safe and supportive environment. Interestingly, it is theorized that this underdeveloped 'sponginess' is why small children are able to learn new languages more quickly than older children and adults. They are, in a very literal way, absorbing information raw, unhampered by the processing and reason of a more mature brain.[7]

Expecting young children to have the maturity and self-control to overcome this God-given survival instinct is unrealistic. Threatening, punishing, or even reasoning with them while their higher brain functions are suppressed is futile and actually just adds more stress to the situation (more stress = fuel on the tantrum-fire!).

What they really need is help...

- First, help coping with their big emotions

- Then, help reconnecting with their source of safety and security (you!)

- And last, help processing the problem that sent them into a maelstrom of emotion in the first place.

Punishing them, yelling at them, sending them to the putting them in time-out disconnects them even further from their source of security and not only delays a resolution of the issue, but misses an opportunity to equip them with the tools they need to handle future problems.

This is where the Three C's of gentle discipline come into play.

Connection:

- Remaining present and supportive until they are able to calm down enough to accept your help

- Drawing them close when they're ready (time-in)

Communication:

- Validating their emotions by labeling them and empathizing (i.e. "You're sad because we have to leave the park. I'm sad, too. The park is fun!")

- Offering words to help them express their frustrations using reflective language (i.e. "It's hard to do things we don't like, isn't it?")

Cooperation:

- Helping them move on by redirecting their attention to the future (i.e. "When we get home we're going to make a snack. Would you like grapes or bananas today?")

- Modeling coping skills and self-control by calming your own reaction to their meltdown and helping them process their big emotions

These are all ways of reconnecting with your toddler or preschooler to help them successfully navigate their present difficulty as well as to cope with difficulties they're confronted with in the future.

One effective tool for use in helping little ones cope with big emotions is a Calm-Me-Jar made from small, round, plastic bottles such as Aquapod™ water bottles. They are perfect for small hands to shake and manhandle to their heart's content.

To make your own Calm-Me-Jar, fill up a plastic water bottle with warm water and basic craft glitter glue in whatever color you like. You can add some extra glitter and a drop of food coloring to customize your glitter jar to your child's tastes, and then when you have the look you want, be sure to hot glue the top on to prevent spills.

When my little ones have meltdowns, or, if I can catch it, before they reach that point, I pull out one of the Calm-Me-Jars and shake it up and just let them hold it while I hold them (when they are ready to be held) and talk or sing quietly. When I feel their body relaxing and their breathing slow down, I might say something like, "It's sad when we can't have a toy, isn't it?" or whatever else will reflect what they seem to be unable to express.

When an older preschooler or early elementary-aged child has a meltdown, or, again, before if I can catch it, I first connect, "I'm here. I can see you're upset. How can I help?" and listen as they try to verbalize their feelings. If they're having trouble with the words, instead of immediately supplying the words for them, I'll offer them a Calm-Me-Jar and ask if they'd like to show me how they're feeling. They will often shake the Calm-Me-Jar vigorously while jumping up and down and twisting all around, which is a great physical outlet for their intense feelings. I watch until I see their movements slowing and their breathing evening out, and when they've calmed just enough to hear me, I quietly talk them through the calming process, "Look at all that fairy dust bouncing around like crazy! I bet that's how it feels inside when you're so upset. Look at how it's starting to slow down and settle to the bottom. If we breathe really slowly, we can feel ourselves settling like the fairy dust. Want to try it with me?" Then, if there are any behavior issues we need to address, we'll work through those afterward when they're calm, connected, and capable of interacting and understanding.

Here's an example of how Calm-Me-Jars are helpful in 'listening between the lines' to my children's behavior so I can meet them where they are and help them process their big feelings:

> My five-year-old is a tiny girl with BIG emotions, and she really likes using Calm-Me-Jars to work through her feelings. We've put several together such as a silvery one she named *Goodnight Moon*, a light blue one she named *Nemo Under the Sea*, a pink one she named *Hello Kitty Princess Ballerina*, and a dark blue one she named *Starry, Starry Night*. When she is mad at one of her siblings, she'll often bring me one of her Calm-Me-Jars (*Goodnight Moon* is a favorite in the evening!) and work out some of her upset physically by shaking the jar like crazy while she jumps up and down and tells me how mad she is. When she's a bit calmer, we'll have a little cuddle and watch the glitter settle while saying goodnight to the moon, all the furniture, and whatever other silliness we come up with until she's calm. If there's a discipline issue or she needs some help working things out with a sibling, we'll work through it at that point because I know that's when she can hear me and really process what I'm saying. If she chooses *Starry, Starry Night* we might sing *Twinkle, Twinkle Little Star* or step outside and see if there are any stars out yet. If she decides on *Hello Kitty Princess Ballerina* she'll often dance her frustrations away while shaking her Calm-Me-Jar. And if she picks out *Nemo Under the Sea* we'll 'speak whale' like Dory from *Finding Nemo*[8] or we'll make fishy faces at each other until we're both giggling.

As you can see, my feisty little girl's choice of Calm-Me-Jar shows me what she needs to do to work through her emotions of the moment, whether it's to act things out physically in acceptable ways or to connect through song or through silliness.

The key is being in tune with your little one enough to understand their personality and work with it instead of against it. My five-year-old is spunky and silly, so having a long, serious talk would drive her crazy and accomplish nothing. We quickly decide together how she'll approach whatever the problem was the next time she encounters it, and then she's ready to move on, whereas when some of my older ones were little they really liked to talk things through (and still do!). My toddler, on the other hand, doesn't have tantrums because that simply isn't part of her own unique personality, but she's still fascinated by her Calm-Me-Jar and loves to sit with me and watch the "pintess faywe dut" ("princess fairy dust") glitter settle when she's feeling a bit cranky or out-of-sorts.

Remember, there is no cure for tantrums because they are simply a normal result of a normal developmental stage of childhood. Trying to avoid tantrum triggers (tiredness, hunger, overstimulation, etc.) is always a good first step, along with remaining in-tune, responsive, and available, but when all else fails and a tantrum does occur, reacting with an adult tantrum is tantamount to throwing fuel on a toddler-tantrum-fire. So instead of losing it when your little one loses it, take an adult time-out, breathe deeply to gain control of your own emotions, and then grab the Three C's of gentle discipline from your parenting toolbox and work with your child, not against them.

"Reactors react to a crisis with a meltdown. Responders respond to a crisis with help. To raise a mature, stable adult, be a first responder, not a nuclear reactor!"

Chapter 9

When Things Get Physical:
Hitting, Throwing, Kicking and Biting

Toddlers and preschoolers are still in the early stages of learning to communicate verbally. Add to that the fact that they have little-to-no impulse control and very immature social skills, and you've got a recipe for an instinctive physical response (i.e. hitting, kicking, biting, hair pulling, throwing things, etc.) to situations when they are frustrated, angry, excited, scared, or just tired and out-of-sorts.

Many parents who practice gentle discipline wonder where their little one picked up the behavior, not realizing that it is a normal and age-appropriate reaction, albeit an undesirable one. Very often parents are advised to spank their child to train them not to hit others, especially those who are smaller and weaker than they are.

The concept of using consequences, physical or otherwise, as a deterrent for hitting is based on the misconception that small children have the capacity for forethought (i.e. "If I hit, I will get in trouble. Therefore I will not hit.") and that they are choosing to disobey. As mentioned in the last chapter, though, the prefrontal cortex, where reasoning, logic, and forethought take place, is highly immature in toddlers and preschoolers and actually doesn't develop fully until the mid-twenties.[6] Small children act instinctively and impulsively even when not stressed simply because that is what they are developmentally capable of, but when they are stressed, even the small amount of self-control they may have attained flies right out the window, and before they know it they've reacted physically to their stress.

The plain truth is, though, that even if punishment was effective as a deterrent, a gentle response to physical aggression is literally the only response that a parent can make that won't actually reinforce the aggression.[9] Responding with counter-aggression by powering-up on a child, whether physically or verbally, merely reinforces the idea that 'might makes right' and that whoever is the dominant figure at any given moment has the right to force others to bend to their will.

Obviously, parents who practice gentle discipline don't believe that hitting a child to teach them not to hit others is an appropriate or even logical option. But knowing that they don't want to resort to physical punishment and knowing what to do instead are two different things entirely.

So, what other options does a gentle parent have when confronted with a little one who has started lashing out physically whether from anger, frustration, or excitement?

1. Supervision! Supervision! Supervision! When you have a child who is acting out physically, it's vital to remain in visual contact with them whenever they are with other children. Easier said than done, I know, but it's important not to leave small children alone with a child who is struggling with physical aggression. Some steps you can take are to either take the child with you when you have to leave the room, take the other child/children with you, or use baby gates to section off areas where you can separate the children to play (in a non-punitive manner) when you have to be out of visual range momentarily.

2. Intervention. Consistent intervention by an observant parent, preferably before the situation escalates to physical aggression, is essential in order to protect the other children. When you see your child heading toward a physical response to a situation, reminding them to use their words or offering a solution to the problem will often help avert a lash out. If your child

has already started to become physical, but hasn't fully escalated, reminding them to "Use your gentle hands" will give them a little head's up that they are headed in the wrong direction and give them an opportunity to redirect themselves. Suggesting alternative options will equip your child with the tools they need to handle their feelings in acceptable ways.

3. Prevention. If scratching or biting are issues be sure to keep your little one's nails trimmed and try to stay on top of teething pain. When it comes to teething, small children are frequently either dealing with swollen gums from a tooth starting to come in or one that has just come in, so being aware of that and using amber necklaces, keeping a supply of damp, frozen washcloths available, and giving a bit of ibuprofen when needed are good preventatives to biting.

4. Remind and redirect. If hitting, biting, scratching, etc. are the result of over-exuberance, consistently reminding a little one to "Use your gentle hands. Can you show me your gentle hands?" or that "Teeth are for smiling, not biting. Can you show me your smile?" and offering specific alternatives such as clapping their hands to show their excitement will help to redirect them to more appropriate expressions of their big emotions.

5. Respect. Respecting a child's possessions helps them to share by offering them the chance to choose. Feeling more in control of what does or does not need to be shared is a proactive step toward a child feeling more in control of their body and impulses. You might allow their room to be off limits to their siblings or possibly have a 'special' toy box where they can keep a select few toys that they don't have to share, but can only play with in their room or when the other children are sleeping or otherwise occupied. If a situation arises

where they aren't willing to share something, they can have the option to choose to put that toy in the 'special' toy box, but will need to decide which toy to take out of the box to share in its place.

6. Outlets. Children who feel out-of-control need outlets for their big feelings. If they're angry, they can go to their room and punch a bop bag or go outside and throw or kick a ball around. But if they're headed toward a meltdown, they may need help processing their feelings, and a Calm-Me-Jar and time-in (see Chapter Eight) may be the best option.

7. Practice. Role playing can be helpful with a child who repeatedly lapses into physical aggression. You can take turns being the 'hit-ee' and 'hitter' (avoid using labels such as 'victim' and 'aggressor' with your child) and show them different ways of handling situations that you know have caused them difficulties in the past.

8. Silliness. One of my favorite tools when dealing with toddler's and preschooler's aggression is playing the 'I'm the boss of you, hands!' game (can also be used for teeth, feet, etc.) in which I remind them that they are the 'boss' of their hands and ask them to tell their hands what they can or cannot do. (i.e. Me: "What are you going to tell your hands if they try to snatch a toy?" Child: "I'll tell them, 'No way, hands! I'm the boss of you!'") Little ones love the idea of being the boss and generally respond well to this type of play.

9. More silliness. For younger, non-verbal children who may not be ready for the "I'm the boss of you, hands!" game yet, if they've hit, pinched, snatched, etc. try 'checking' to see if they have gentle hands by exaggeratedly examining their hands and then kissing

each palm and declaring, "Yep, that's a gentle hand, all right!" The positive, declarative statement will help them to develop a positive self-image and set the foundation for self-control as they grow up believing that, yes, they are good and gentle little people!

10. Modeling. If your child has already hit someone, you will need to first address the injured child's needs. If you're angry with your child for hitting, and you very well may be, it's okay to share that with them in a calm voice and let them know that you need a moment to console the injured child and to calm down before you will be ready to talk with them. What you are actually doing is modeling self-control and coping mechanisms, important components for your child to learn in order to master their impulse to lash out.

11. Teaching empathy. Reflect what the other person might be feeling, "It hurts your sister when you scratch her. Why don't we go ask her if she's okay? If she has an owie, we might need to get a bandage for her." It's very intriguing for little ones to feel like they can 'fix' something, and often the idea that they have that kind of power makes them more likely to feel they have the power to use their gentle hands, too. The positive impact of learning to think and care about the feelings of others, though, is the real power that will enable them to begin to control the impulse to lash out.

12. Verbalize. Offering words to express your child's feelings of anger or frustration when they have lashed out (i.e. "I see that you don't want to share the ball. That makes you angry. I'm sorry you're angry, but I can't let you hit. What can you do instead of hitting when you're angry?") will help your child learn how to verbalize their feelings over time instead of simply acting on them as well as reminding them of the options you've provided for them to redirect their big feelings into acceptable outlets.

13. A place for time-outs. When a toy is misused (i.e. thrown, used to hit, etc.) and a gentle redirection has already been given, another option is to try the 'Time-Out Toy Box.' Little ones generally find the concept of a toy being put in time-out rather humorous and go along with the removal without a fuss. When your child decides that the toy is ready to behave, you can have your little one tell the toy it has to listen to them because they are the boss. Again, humor is a great communicator! Remember, though to listen and be flexible. If the removal of a toy brings about a strong negative response, a time-in with your little one might be needed (see Chapter Eight). Remaining in-tune with your child will help you to read the situation and respond appropriately.

14. Expectations. It's important in all aspects of parenting to frequently take a step back and examine your expectations to make sure that they are reasonable in regard to your child's age, developmental stage, temperament, etc. Unrealistic expectations can put significant pressure on a child and cause a great deal of frustration and stress which can lead to aggressive behaviors as well as conflict in your parent/child relationship.

15. Honesty. If physical punishment has been a part of your parenting, removing that entirely from your parenting toolbox is a great start toward easing some of the anger, stress, and frustration that is fueling your child's aggression. Being honest with your child about your own struggles with handling things physically as well as apologizing for using threats, intimidation, and physical pain to control them in the past will begin the healing process in your relationship.

Always try to keep in mind that behaviors are communication. Listening 'between the lines' to your child's aggression will help you to discern whether your child's behavior is communicating an unmet need such as hunger, a nap, or attention (Yes, attention is a valid need!) or if they are communicating a big emotion that they're having trouble processing or if they are simply out of their depth and need an adult to help them handle a situation. Children are actually great communicators, just not necessarily verbally. It's up to us adults to 'listen' carefully, empathetically, and calmly to our children's behavior and then offer them our gentle guidance, wisdom, and support.

Chapter 10

Testing the Boundaries

Challenging behavior in our children can be really...well, challenging! How do you 'handle' a child who suddenly refuses to wear shoes or sit in her carseat/seatbelt or eat, period? Here are some tips to help you regain that snuggly, loving relationship you used to enjoy before your cuddly baby became a...gulp...PERSON!

- Remove the word 'handle' from your parenting vocabulary entirely. Your child isn't a lion to be tamed or a dog to be trained. Your child is a person, an individual with thoughts, interests, concerns, wants, and needs that are totally separate from yours. Respecting our children as separate individuals not only models the value we need to place on others in our homes and communities, but also sets the stage for a mutually respectful relationship in the teen years and beyond.

- Slow down. Often simplifying our lives is the key to simplifying our parenting issues. Rushing a child from one activity to the next doesn't expand their horizons; it stunts their creativity and inherent zest for life which are the building blocks of a life-long love of learning. When they dig their heels in, pay attention. They are trying to communicate a very deep need for time and space to learn about the world, to play and grow, and to just 'be.'

- Small children have very little control over their lives, and the more powerless they feel, the more likely they are to make eating, getting dressed, going to the potty, etc. a battle of wills. Giving choices, engaging your child in making plans, and being flexible and responsive on a daily basis are good 'proactive' parenting, but little people are notorious for their awkward timing in deciding to suddenly assert their independence! Be prepared for those challenging moments by deciding ahead of time how you will respond.

- Listen, listen, listen. The first question parents ask me is almost always, "How do I get my child to listen?" And my first response is usually, "How well do you listen?" As Ralph Waldo Emerson so aptly put it, "What you do speaks so loud that I cannot hear what you say." In other words, our children learn best by imitation. If every time our little ones ask for our attention we say, "Just a minute," then we cannot expect instant attention from them. If when they speak to us our eyes constantly stray back to our computers and iPhones, we should not be surprised if they have a hard time paying attention to us. Listening is a two-way street that starts and ends with us, the adults.

- Boundaries are our friends. Many people believe that gentle parenting is a form of un-parenting, but nothing could be further from the truth. Gentle parenting is involved parenting—interactive, engaged, active parenting. It takes focused attention, planning, participation, research, and so much more to be an empathetic, responsive parent who is in tune with their child's needs and who is prepared to make whatever sacrifices are necessary to meet those needs. That said, in any home, like in any civilized society, boundaries are necessary for everyone's safety and comfort. It is in the choosing and maintaining of those boundaries that gentle parenting distinguishes itself. In a gently parented home, boundaries are focused on guiding rather than controlling children and are maintained through empathetic and creative resolutions rather than harsh punitive consequences.

- Watch your attitude. Do you have angry eyes? A sharp tone? Do you issue commands and demand compliance? Do you sigh and roll your eyes when frustrated with your little one? All of these things contribute to creating resistance in children. Really, who wants to cooperate with someone who is demanding, impatient, sarcastic, and angry? Does feeling like a burden or a failure motivate *you*? Think about how you like to be treated by authority figures (supervisors, law enforcement, etc.) and then treat your children the way you want to be treated. This not only reduces challenging behavior, but also models The Golden Rule: "Do to others as you want them to do to you." An excellent life lesson!

- Keep in mind, the most challenging, independent children tend to be the ones who need the most intentional parental reconnection. Strong will = Strong need! It is often the children gifted with the strongest wills who identify most closely with their parents, oddly enough. While there is no denying how difficult it can be to raise a strong-willed child, seeing the purpose behind the behavior can make the journey much more manageable. Try to view their seemingly constant testing as them doing 'research' on you, seeing where your strengths and weaknesses are, and discovering all the ins and outs of being you. Also, taking the time to explain why you make the decisions you do, why you said this, why you didn't say that, answering the endless questions patiently and openly, can alleviate some of the challenging behavior by offering them insights into who you are without them having to 'dig' it out of you!

Remember that repetition is key. Parenting isn't a series of destinations and rest stops. It's a dance…two steps forward, one step back…one step forward, two steps back. That's just part of the rhythm as you dance to the melody of childhood with your little one. Don't get tripped up by the details. Just enjoy the dance!

Chapter 11

Parenting in Public

You're sitting in a restaurant waiting the prerequisite ten to fifteen minutes for your food to be served, chatting quietly with your spouse and two-year-old, when *it* happens, that dreaded moment that every parent fears...the sudden switch from table companion to meltdown mayhem when life as you and every patron, staff member, and passerby know it is turned inside out and upside down.

That moment is known as 'Toddler Time' which is aptly named because it is, in fact, all about time from the perspective of a toddler. That insignificant ten to fifteen minute waiting period for food to arrive is actually *eons* in toddler time, eons of hunger, eons of boredom, eons of stillness, eons of being expected to act like the adult that they are years and years (*eons!*) away from becoming. But you really don't want to be housebound for all of those eons, right? And yet more and more public places are becoming child un-friendly with snarky signs saying they'll give your child an espresso and a pony if you don't control them, or charge you extra if you dare to enter their establishment and support their business with your hard-earned money, or even flat out ban you altogether if you bring 'the beast' out in public with you!

And what about those hazy, lazy summer days at the park with the laughter of children floating in the air, mommies wearing sleeping babies in their carriers while chatting and keeping eagle eyes on their precious little monkeys dangling from brightly colored jungle-gyms, when the dreaded moment suddenly hits, and all goes quiet as every eye turns toward the poor soul who called out those awful, awful words, "*It's time to go!*" The words echo against the lowering sky, which has conveniently decided to threaten rain just to add to the sheer madness of the moment, and then the shrieking begins. In toddler time, an hour at the park is gone in the blink of an eye, and fun things like being strapped into car seats and baths and naps awaiting at home just add insult to injury.

So what's a parent to do?

Here are a few preemptive tools for your gentle parenting toolbox:

1. Gather a few special 'quiet' toys and keep them in a Quiet Bag in the car. To keep their novelty value, only get them out when you go into a store or restaurant and let your little one play with one toy at a time until it's time to go, saving one last special toy for the car ride home. Some ideas for stocking your Quiet Bag are

    - felt busy books

    - playdoh

    - picture books

    - white-erase boards

    - coloring books

    - small, unlined notebooks

    - crayons or washable markers

    - mini stuffed animals

    - small play figures such as superheroes, dollhouse dolls, cars, trucks, etc.

    - chunky, age-appropriate puzzles

    - Calm-Me-Jars (see Chapter Eight)

2. Making a habit out of wearing your little one or letting them ride in a cart or stroller while in stores and keeping them happily occupied while secured in a highchair or on your lap when in restaurants are proactive steps that will help prevent issues with running around and getting into things.

3. Keeping your little person occupied is always a good place to start, but if yelling or screaming still become an issue, try responding with a whispered question or two. It's pretty much irresistible for little ones to quiet down to hear what you're saying, and even better if what you're saying is super silly..."I think my nose went outside for a walk." (with a conspiratorial 'shared secret' look) "Could you check for me to see if it's back yet?" (crossing your eyes to see for yourself)

4. With the dreaded leaving-the-park issue, try bringing snacks your small one loves, and instead of saying "Time to go!" try saying "Snack time!" and describe the yumminess waiting for them, all the while gently guiding them to the car. Or brainstorm with your little one ahead of time to come up with a fun activity to do after the park like playing a favorite game together or stopping by the library to pick up a new book to read together. The idea is to involve your toddler in the planning so they feel like they have some control over their lives and also to have something fun to look forward to that will help them through transitions (which are always hard for little ones).

5. Don't forget to pack your 'funnybone' for a back-up plan! Humor is a powerful parenting tool, and car seats presented as rocket ships to the moon, shared naptimes (parents can always use the extra sleep!) on marshmallow planets, highchair-bound movie directors with mommy and daddy as the actors, and shopping

carts cars that continually stall and need to be fixed by their little riders are all inventive ways of keeping little people too busy and happy to meltdown. (Not to mention that these are great ways to reconnect with your little one and remember just how adorable they really are!)

6. Actively work at avoiding confrontations and meltdowns by giving choices, staying engaged, listening to your child, and paying attention to triggers such as hunger, tiredness, sickness, etc. When our parenting goals shift from meeting needs and guiding actions to controlling our children, they invariably rebel and the battle is on, not a happy circumstance at any time, but especially difficult to handle in public! (And, in the long run, that makes for an 'us against them' relationship that sets the stage for an unhappy home, particularly when the teen years arrive.)

Chapter 12

Crying Wolf: Don't Be an Old Yeller!

"YELLING silences your message. Speak quietly so your children can hear your words, not just your voice."

Remember the story of the little boy who cried wolf? It's a classic tale that parents through the years have told their children when their children have lied or exaggerated. As the story goes, a little shepherd boy wanted to get the attention of the villagers, so he ran into the village shouting, "Wolf! Wolf!" so that the villagers would come running and try to help save his sheep from the wolf. After a few false alarms, though, an actual wolf did attack the sheep, but the villagers ignored the cries of "Wolf" from the little shepherd boy because they no longer believed that there was a real emergency. The entire flock was lost, and the little shepherd boy learned a hard lesson.

It seems that is an even harder lesson for parents to learn, though. Ask a roomful of parents what the one thing they'd most like to change about their own parenting is, and you're likely to hear an overwhelming majority shout, "I need to stop yelling!"

The thing is, yelling at your children constantly is the equivalent of lying to them, or, at the very least, severely exaggerating. When you yell, you are communicating that there is an emergency, and when you yell about everything you are communicating that *everything* is an emergency. The problem with that is exactly the problem that our young yeller from the wolf story encountered—over time people learn to tune-out the messenger and grow deaf to the message.

Consider:

> *There was a young family with a father who had a yelling issue. He yelled if there were toys in the middle of the floor. He yelled if everyone wasn't ready to leave on time. He yelled if someone spilled a drink. He yelled*

if someone forgot their shoes at home. One day his little girl, after being yelled at for the umpteenth time that day, looked at him and, in all earnestness, said, "Daddy, you need to stop being a 'leller.'" The problem this father faced was that, in addition to the damage he was doing to his relationship with his daughter, his ability to communicate in a real crisis was drastically diminished. Since his yelling communicated that everything *was a crisis, his constant panic mode made his little girl immune to that note of panic in his voice that would normally alert her to a real crisis such as running into traffic or touching a hot stove, leading to some potentially dangerous situations.*

Another family had a similar problem, but it was the mother who literally shrieked until she lost her voice on a daily basis over such 'emergencies' as missing socks and unmade beds. Her children learned at very young ages to tune her out and, as a result, her family was in a constant state of chaos and she was a nervous wreck.

Each of these young parents learned the hard way that yelling did the exact opposite of what it was intended to do. It didn't get their message across more clearly or forcefully. It instead silenced their message and weakened their effectiveness as parents.

If you find yourself yelling, or before you yell if you can catch yourself, take a parental time-out, breathe deeply to regain control of yourself, and remind yourself that everything is not a crisis, then work on approaching whatever the issue is with the self-control, maturity, and grace that you'd like your children to emulate. Remember, they are watching, and they are learning, so act like the adult you want them to become.

Chapter 13

Toxic Parenting:
Spanking, Shaming, Threatening, Manipulating

Want to help stop the bullying epidemic? Don't act like a bully. Don't hit, threaten, ignore, isolate, intimidate, ridicule, or manipulate your child. Children really do learn what they live…

I stood, frozen in shock, outside of the upscale bookstore where I would soon be signing my gentle parenting books and chatting with parents about alternatives to punishment-based parenting. A well-dressed young couple I'd spoken with just minutes before in a nearby pizzeria was getting into an expensive SUV several yards away from where I was standing, but the screams were crystal clear.

The young man was leaning over his wife who sat shrinking into her seat as he screamed in her face, "Get in the car! Get in the car!" over and over again. The woman was clearly confused, as was I. She was in the car, though not yet buckled up, so why in the world was the man screaming at his wife to get in? It suddenly dawned on me that what he wanted her to do was put her seatbelt on, but the man was too enraged to even realize that wasn't what he was actually saying.

I glanced down at my little one who was shrinking back in fear and tried to organize my thoughts so I could cross the few yards separating me from the SUV and engage the man in conversation. If nothing else, I thought, reminding him that people were watching might help him to take a moment and compose himself.

But in the next second, the man suddenly yanked his wife out of her seat and landed several stinging blows on her bare skin before flinging her back into her seat, this time screaming at the sobbing woman, "You are

*not in charge! You are not in charge!" He then
slammed her door shut, stomped around to his own
seat, slammed his door, and pealed out of his parking
space.*

*I quickly snapped a picture of the license plate with my
iPhone and called the police to report the domestic
violence I'd just witnessed. They immediately sent out
an officer to track down the endangered woman and
take the man into custody.*

Now here's the real story...

*On a recent book tour I stood, frozen in shock, outside
of the upscale bookstore where I would soon be signing
my gentle parenting books and chatting with parents
about alternatives to punishment-based parenting. A
well-dressed woman and her two small children whom
I'd chatted with just moments before in a nearby
pizzeria were getting into an expensive SUV, but the
screams were crystal clear.*

*The woman was leaning over her toddler and four-
year-old who sat shrinking into their carseats as she
screamed in their faces, "Get in the car! Get in the
car!" at them over and over again. The children were
clearly confused, as was I. They were in their carseats,
though not yet buckled up, so why in the world was the
woman screaming at her children to get in? It suddenly
dawned on me that what she wanted was for the toddler
to put her own arms in the straps, but the mother was
too enraged to even realize that wasn't what she was
actually saying.*

*I glanced down at my little one who was shrinking back
in fear and tried to organize my thoughts so I could
cross the few yards separating me from the SUV and
engage the woman in conversation. If nothing else, I
thought, reminding the mother that people were
watching might help her to take a moment and compose
herself.*

*But in the next second, the woman suddenly yanked her
toddler out of her carseat and landed several stinging
blows to her chubby little legs before flinging her back
into her carseat, this time screaming at the sobbing
child, "You are not in charge! You are not in charge!"
She then roughly buckled the little one in, stomped
around to her own seat, slammed her door, and pealed
out of her parking space.*

*As I stood there staring through tears at the tail lights
speeding away, I realized that if I'd just witnessed a
man doing that to his wife I could call the police who
would intervene immediately because there are laws to
protect adults from domestic violence, but there are no
such laws protecting children in the US.*

My opportunity was lost to touch those small children's lives,
and my heart aches for them. Was the mother just having a bad
day? Was she angry at the snarky pizzeria cashier? Was she
frustrated that dinner was pizza again because she'd been
delayed at work? I don't know, and, honestly, I don't care. If a
man was having a bad day, we wouldn't accept that as an excuse
for domestic violence.

Hitting any human being other than a child is against the law in
the United States where it is legal for parents to hit their children
whenever and wherever and with whatever they want to as long
as it doesn't leave lasting marks and, in nineteen states, for
school officials to hit children with anything from rulers to two
foot long boards. That is not acceptable. In fact, it is outrageous.

Though I know I can't change the world for every child, I am
determined to change the world for as many children as humanly
possible. We don't need new laws. We just need the domestic
violence laws already in place to protect adults to be extended to
protect our most vulnerable, voiceless, voteless citizens, our
children.

Did you know that there is less evidence linking lead exposure
to developmental delays in children and asbestos to cancer than
there is of the short and long-term detrimental effects of
spanking? Study after study has confirmed that spanking (not

just physical abuse, but *any* physical act of correction - smacking, hitting, swatting, slapping, paddling, switching, etc.) is directly linked to *greater* aggression and other behavioral issues, impaired cognitive development, and increased risk of depression and anxiety in childhood as well as long-term mental issues in adulthood.[10] And yet the American public is still reluctant to dismiss the physical punishment of children as an option for parents and school systems.

It is not unusual for public opinion to evolve slowly. Until recent years, husbands hitting their spouses in the US was considered "reasonable chastisement of wives" and "a private family matter" by the courts and by law enforcement even though it has technically been against the law in all fifty states for decades. Now domestic violence in the US is viewed with outrage and abusers with disdain.

While the tide is ever-so-slowly turning regarding public opinion of the physical punishment of children, in excess of eighty-percent of Americans still believe spanking is a necessary part of raising a child according to a survey cited by a UN report. And in the nineteen US states where corporal punishment is still legal in the public school system, wooden paddles are used on children as young as preschool, and parents' permission or notification is often not even required. By contrast, in every branch of the US military and in the US penal system, physical punishment has long been outlawed as it was deemed 'cruel and unusual' and a 'use of excessive force.'[11]

Clearly there is a disconnect when it comes to physical punishment of the most vulnerable and defenseless of our citizens, our children. Even in the face of study after study detailing the detrimental effects of physical punishment on young children, more than ninety-percent of American parents still admit to spanking their toddlers and pre-schoolers,[12] even if they don't believe that it is a good alternative. The responses to a recently released study[10] linking a significantly increased risk of mental illness in adulthood to being spanked as a child point to some possible reasons for that dichotomy:

1."I was spanked, and I turned out okay."

Not everyone who smokes gets lung cancer, but why take the risk?

2. "I don't want to raise a rotten brat!"

Studies link spanking to increased aggression and other behavioral issues, not decreased.

3. "I spank my kids because the Bible commands me to."

Not only is spanking not one of the Ten Commandments, but commanding or even suggesting that parents hit young children is not found anywhere in the Bible. The handful of Old Testament 'rod' and 'training' verses used to support this theory are misinterpreted to refer to physical punishment instead of guidance, and the word translated 'child' in those verses is translated 'young man' in every other instance.

4. "They're my kids, and nobody has the right to tell me how to raise them!"

Our laws are civil agreements as to what is and is not acceptable in our society. We once agreed that slavery was acceptable. Now we know better, and our laws reflect that. As research continues to reveal the detrimental effects of spanking, public opinion will begin to shift and our laws will naturally follow suit. It is the way of a democratic society.

5. "Nothing else works!"

Thoughtful, compassionate, proactive parenting works.

Beyond even the issue of spanking, though, the mindset of controlling children through external forces rather than helping them learn how to and desire to control themselves is where the real changes need to happen. When humans, whether they are adults or children, are pushed, the inbuilt reaction is to push back. When humans are pulled, the inbuilt reaction is to pull back. When they are threatened, intimidated, or shamed, it is only the size and strength of their opponent that results in submission and that submission is temporary. As soon as the opponent is eliminated from the equation, humans will pursue their own course, often more angrily and rebelliously and single-mindedly.

Becoming our children's opponent is not healthy parenting and it doesn't create a healthy parent/child relationship. It creates a destructive dynamic primed for conflict, rebellion, and escalation. Even when parents choose non-violent means to control their children such as isolation (i.e. time-outs) and behavior charts and other punishment/reward tactics, the basic truth is that they are modelling manipulation and coercion and are focused on controlling a child's behavior externally rather than working with them to help them learn to control their own behavior through an internal guidance system.

In parenting there will always be times when your child's behavior doesn't meet your expectations. Recognizing that you are two distinct individuals with differing opinions and plans and wants and needs will help you to work with your child instead of clashing with them and creating an unhealthy dynamic in your relationship. Be aware that unhealed hurts and unforgiveness, even of yourself, will get in the way of a healthy relationship and take the steps you need to take in order to heal your relationship and yourself (see Chapter Fifteen).

Whenever things escalate to the point where you withhold affection and connection in order to punish or try to control behavior, and certainly if you are hitting or if you are hurting your child emotionally through threats, intimidation, and shaming, you can be sure you've stepped off the gentle discipline path. But there is always a way back, and that's through reconnection, owning our mistakes, and starting again. The bottom line is that we cannot control another human being. We can force external obedience temporarily, but only by constantly escalating the threats, emotional manipulations, and punishments which accomplish nothing in the long run and do far greater damage than they are worth.

There is no doubt that the vast majority of parent deeply love their children, but, based on the info experiences they have to work with, are also making the parenting decisions they know how to make. Working with our children instead of against them is a foreign concept to most parents, but therein lies the secret to a peaceful, happy home and the healthy parent/child trust relationship that the Three C's of gentle discipline—Connection, Communication, and Cooperation—are built upon.

Chapter 14

All the 'Right' Parenting Moves

*"I'm an imperfect human raising an imperfect human in an
imperfect world, and that's perfectly okay!"*

Ever have one of those days where you make all the 'right'
parenting moves, but your children still act like children? (Do I
hear a resounding "YES!'? Of course we all have, and a whole
lot more than just one day, too!)

I'm still chuckling over the message that someone sent me in
which they stated that I'd clearly never had a 'problem child'
and wishing me good luck if I ever have more than one child
because then my chances of having said 'problem child' would
increase. For the record, amongst my six children I have two
with sensory issues, one with full-blown Sensory Processing
Disorder, two with ADD, one with Auditory Processing
Disorder, and two who would be labelled 'strong-willed' or
'high-maintenance' or even 'problem children' by people who
want to label children.

The thing that people so often misunderstand is that gentle
parenting is not about stopping our children from being children.
It's about guiding our children through childhood with
gentleness, compassion, and respect. It's about viewing normal
childhood behavior as normal, and working with our children in
developmentally appropriate ways to teach and inspire and
encourage them to become the extraordinary people they were
created to be.

Gentle parenting doesn't cure childhood because childhood isn't
a disease. It doesn't fix children because children aren't broken.
Time passes. Childhood ends. And with the passing of
childhood, children stop acting like children and start acting like
adults. Gentle parenting simply recognizes normal childhood
behaviors as normal and offers gentle guidance to help children
grow into healthy adults.

Life-ready, heart-whole adults who act like adults in overgrown children are born of children who are giv chance to fully embrace their childhood, whose bodies are careu for with respect, and whose hearts are not broken again and again.

And yet, while it's true that our parenting choices have profound immediate and long-term impacts on our children, it's also true that our children aren't simply mirrors of our parenting. Our children are fully separate individuals from ourselves, entirely whole people with wants and needs and hopes and fears and interests and emotions all their own, not to mention their own distinct temperaments and personalities.

Yes, they are always watching, always learning, always imitating us, but they are also just as stunningly and spectacularly unpredictable as falling stars. So when we've done our parental best, tried our hardest, met needs, cuddled, soothed, played, listened, and guided, and our baby still cries or our toddler still has a meltdown or our child still makes an unfortunate choice, let's simply stay close, calmly offering our comforting arms, reassuring presence, and unconditional love while resting in the peaceful assurance that our little stars are simply having a human moment. [From *Two Thousand Kisses a Day: Gentle Parenting Through the Ages and Stages*]

The thing is, parenting has nothing to do with perfection. Perfection isn't even the goal, not for us, not for our children. Learning together to live well in an imperfect world, loving each other despite or even because of our imperfections, and growing as humans while we grow our little humans, those are the goals of gentle parenting. So don't ask yourself at the end of the day if you did everything right. Ask yourself what you learned and how well you loved, then grow from your answer. That is perfect parenting.

I've had those days where my extraordinary little people have acted like children, where I made all the 'right' parenting moves, and yet it turned out to be a frustrating, tiring, out-of-sorts kind of day for all of us. And that's perfectly okay with me. We all have days like that. We simply start over again the next day.

And the next. And every day after that. That's just how crazy, beautiful, wonderful life with children goes.

Chapter 15

Hurting Parents, Hurting Children

It is the nature of a child to behave childishly. That means childish behavior is normal for children. Not so for adults. When we find ourselves reacting to our children's normal childhood behavior with childish outbursts of our own—hitting, demanding our own way, name calling, etc.—that reveals areas we need to grow in our own lives so that we can respond with the true nature of an adult...with maturity, wisdom, confidence, and compassion.

Examining our negative reactions to our children and identifying where they come from can be difficult because they are so often rooted in our own negative childhood experiences and unmet needs.

A difficult childhood can leave us as adults with a lack of self-regulation skills that cause a constant, underlying stress. If as a child we were trained to be controlled by others, we may always feel a bit out-of-control when there's no one to control us except ourselves. If we were abused or neglected, we may have buried hurts so deeply that we don't even realize they are still there. The result may be that we became an adult who is constantly angry without knowing why or who is a control freak or who can't handle change or even an adult who has no self-control at all. Unfortunately, it often isn't until we become a parent ourselves that these hurts begin to surface unexpectedly in outbursts of anger toward our children or an inability to bond with our children or a myriad of other subtle and not-so-subtle ways.

Seeing our childhood hurts reflected in our children often has the unexpected result of creating anger toward our children in us as well as a resistance to changing the cause of the hurt. That is the hurt child in us lashing out, as children often do when they are in pain.

Working toward forgiveness and peace with our past in those areas is essential so that we can stop the cycle and not pass along that baggage to our children. Recognizing our childhood hurts and unmet needs, isolating those feelings, and dealing with them with the adult emotional maturity that we now have allows us to process, forgive, and move on so that we don't repeat the past with our own children.

That is easier said than done, but it is doable, and it is well worth the emotional investment. Working through our childhood hurts is about forgiving so we can unload our baggage into the past where it belongs instead of unloading it onto our children. Forgiving doesn't mean trying to convince ourselves that the person or persons who hurt us weren't at fault or were right to do (or not do) what they did. It means honestly acknowledging their faults and flaws and honestly acknowledging the hurt that resulted. It also means examining our own humanness and failings so we can acknowledge that we, too, aren't perfect. And it means consciously, intentionally, and consistently choosing to let go of the hurt, put down the baggage, and walk away into a brighter, healthier future.

Healing our own hurts is vital to becoming the parent we want to be, but we may also need to work on changing our mindset from feeling like we need to control our children to wanting to help our children learn to control themselves. When we are focused on controlling our children, we can end up feeling unheard and frustrated, which not only tends to result in making our children also feel unheard and frustrated (passing along our baggage), but also inevitably taps into our own childhood hurts all over again, and then we lash out as hurting children will do. Approaching an anger issue from both sides by healing our hurts and changing our mindset gives us more tools to work with to solve our parenting issues.

The thing is, most parenting mistakes don't come from a lack of love. They come from a lack of understanding. Moving toward understanding ourselves and healing our childhood hurts will help us to move toward understanding and healing our children. We are all human, and we all get angry at times, but doing the work of growing our inner child up into a self-regulated adult will help us to respond with wisdom and compassion to our children instead of reacting to them with harsh punishments and hurtful words.

And we always need to keep in mind that guilt is a destructive emotion, so instead of holding onto guilt, we need to let our love lead us to listen more deeply, understand more fully, connect more securely, forgive more freely, communicate more clearly, and respond more gently. Every day is a new beginning. If we make each day better than the last, we'll give our children the gift of a lifetime…a healthy, happy childhood.

Chapter 16

The Gift of a Strong-Willed Child

There are some children who are born into the world with the incredible life-gift of a strong will and an indomitable spirit. These children are often deeply misunderstood, and there are rows of books lining bookstore shelves with instructions about how to break their will, how to subdue their spirit, how to force their obedience. What an incredible loss of leadership, passion, and insight this world suffers when parents follow these punitive parenting practices. Not only can we parent these gifted children with gentleness and respect, but the gifts we get in return are priceless!

Take a look at some of the common descriptions used when referring to the characteristics of a strong-willed child:

Demanding, Insistent, Stubborn, Bossy, Cocky, Difficult, Challenging, Fixated, Contrary, Rebellious, Defiant

Now look at some of the common characteristics of adults who are world leaders, CEO's, entrepreneurs, innovators, world-class athletes, and the like:

Decisive, Determined, Persistent, Authoritative, Confident, Valiant, Gutsy, Committed, Resourceful, Nonconforming, Bold

Note that the characteristics are the same, but the characterizations are negative when applied to a child and positive when applied to an adult.

Other characteristics of strong-willed children that coincide with the characteristics of adult leaders in their fields are:

- They are typically highly creative and intelligent.

- They are usually passionate and intense in their interests and beliefs.

- They often have an insatiable need to know 'why.'

- They typically learn by doing.

- They tend to have an intense need to test the status quo.

- They are typically highly perfection-oriented, but often that is focused on their expectations of themselves instead of others.

- They tend to need high levels of validation.

- They usually have an intense need to be heard.

- They often have a strong need for emotional safety.

- They tend to be resistant to change unless they feel like they have some control over the change.

- They are often highly sensitive.

- They are typically intensely focused on their latest project or interest.

- They tend to be conscientious and highly committed.

- They are usually intensely independent.

While there's no doubt that it's a challenge having a child who seems to challenge everything, there are ways to work with them rather than against them to preserve and nurture their unique gifts. Maintaining a healthy parent/child relationship is vital as you work to find a balance between setting limits with your richly spirited child while not limiting their freedom to stretch and grow and develop into the person they were created to be.

The key to preserving your trust relationship with your child is remaining calm and present and supportive, even while setting and maintaining reasonable boundaries. It is helpful to remember that the most strong-willed children tend to be the ones who identify the most strongly with their parents. So instead of viewing their seemingly constant challenges as defiance or attempts to thwart authority, work to parent from a place of understanding that your strong-willed child is actually on a discovery mission and is doing endless 'research' on you by testing and retesting and digging and chiseling to discover all of your quirks and foibles and ups and downs and strengths and weaknesses. This kind of testing isn't negative unless you make it into a battle of wills instead of responding with gentle, respectful guidance. Taking this stance will help you to keep from seeing the challenges as personal insults and, instead, see the challenges as attempts to learn and grow and understand.

There is no doubt, though, that parenting a child with the gift of a strong will is a constant exercise in patience and self-regulation. The personal growth you will experience is invaluable as you seek to parent with empathy and wisdom and compassion, but it can be draining and will often stretch you far, far out of your comfort zone. Knowing that and being prepared for it will help you cope with the inevitable stresses, and being ready ahead of time with some specific strategies for handling the challenges will help you to respond calmly and effectively.

This is a good place to revisit the Three C's of gentle discipline—Connection, Communication, and Cooperation.

Connection ~ Maintaining a secure connection with your spirited child is vital. It is the springboard from which all of your interactions with your child will originate, and it is the touchstone to which you will both return, again and again and again, when your relationship gets strained and stained and stretched.

- Play word games, board games, rough-and-tumble outdoor games, silly face in the mirror games. Play is the language of childhood, so make sure to speak your child's language every day.

- Laugh together. Humor is an undervalued parenting tool. But it lowers defenses, inspires smiles, brings people together, and reconnects hearts.

- Read storybooks, chapter books, travel brochures, encyclopedias, anything that will inspire you to dream together, talk, plan, get excited, share interests.

- Focus more on who your child is than on what your child does. Remember, you're growing a person, not fixing a problem. So make sure to spend time getting to know the person, not just the child. It doesn't have to cost anything. Just walk together, talk together, share ice cream cones, spot shapes in the clouds, and enjoy each other.

Communication ~ Children have their own 'inner world' of thoughts and plans and problems and worries and hopes and dreams that are occupying their time and attention, so a lack of cooperation is often simply the result of having a different agenda than we do. Getting some insight into that 'inner world' is key in guiding and growing them respectfully.

- Listen with your heart. Listen 'between the lines' to what your child is communicating through their behavior. Listen and listen and listen some more. That is always, always the first step in communicating with your child.

- Reflect, connect, and redirect. Reflect what you hear, whether it's communicated by your child's behavior or their words. This not only validates their emotions and lets them know that you hear and understand them, but it also helps them to understand their own emotions. For instance, if your child is upset that he can't have a cookie after brushing his teeth for bedtime, try saying, "I hear you. You're upset because you want a cookie." Then reestablish your connection, "I like cookies, too!" and offer a solution, "How about we go pick out the two best cookies and put them in a special container that we can take to the park in the morning?"

- Don't take non-compliance as a personal insult. A strong-willed child is very much their own person with their own agenda. Focus on inviting cooperation instead of demanding obedience. Whether it's staying in bed or cleaning up or whatever the issue, make it a team effort and come up with a game plan ahead of time. For example, you could say, "You seem to be having trouble staying in bed at night. What do you think would help you to be more ready to go to sleep when it's time for bed?" or "It's important to pick up our things so they don't get broken, let's put on the timer and work together for ten minutes and see who gets the most picked up."

- Make a firm commitment not to resort to punishments to control behavior. The resentment that comes from being punished absolves children in their own minds of responsibility. It doesn't teach them responsibility, and resentment can actually cause a lot of the behaviors you are trying to avoid.

- Communicate daily, outwardly to your child and inwardly to yourself, the positive aspects of your child's personality. When the focus is on 'fixing' a child, they get the message that they are somehow broken, and that is not a healthy self-image to take into adulthood.

- 'No' is not a complete thought. It is an imperative, a command. It doesn't teach. It tells. If you want your child to learn to think like an adult, take the time to explain your adult thinking.

- Remember that children, especially when they are upset, open 'conversations' through their behavior, and it's up to us, the only adults in the relationship, to gently guide them toward continuing those conversations verbally as well as equipping them with the resources to be able to do so.

- Also keep in mind that the social mores of rudeness simply aren't inborn and don't apply to early interactions with our children. They are learned by imitating how we as parents behave. Politeness is a heart issue that cannot be imposed by the will of another unless we want it to only be an external façade instead of a heartfelt courtesy. Helping your strong-willed child learn to speak kindly means speaking kindly to your child as well as offering guidance when they've been rude such as saying, "That is not a nice tone of voice" or "That isn't a kind thing to say" and then offering a do-over "Can you try saying that to me again more nicely? I'll always try my best to be nice to you, and I would like you to try to do the same for me." (see Appendix B for more ideas)

Cooperation ~ Always keep at the forefront of your parenting goals that you are seeking thoughtful cooperation, not mindless compliance. That way you will remember to treat your child as a thoughtful individual with ideas and needs and feelings of their own instead of a mindless drone there to do your bidding.

- Set clear limits and explain them in age-appropriate terms. Remember, if you want to invite cooperation, you have to actually issue the invitation to cooperate!

- Limit the number of limits. Spirited children are often stressed children simply because of their own intense emotions and reactions to things, so set them up for success by keeping your limits few and clear and by maintaining them consistently.

- Make sure to let your child have a voice in determining the limits so they feel like they have some control over their lives and so they feel some ownership over the limits.

- Brainstorm together ways of helping everyone to work together. Some ideas are to come up with hand signals or words that remain your little secret codes to indicate when it's time to leave the park or to do homework or to dial the activity level or noise volume down a few notches.

- Invite cooperation by creating daily routines together. Don't be surprised if your child ends up being the one who is a stickler for following the routine, even to the point of nagging *you* to follow it. These gifted children tend to be all-in, fully focused and committed, and they'll expect you to be the same!

- Cooperate with your child's needs and personality by working with them rather than against them. For instance, if you know that your child has a hard time leaving a project, give them plenty of time to find a good stopping point when you need them to leave it for a while. Or if you know that your child has a hard time following directions at bedtime, try writing or drawing the tasks that need to be done (i.e. toothbrushing, pajamas, etc.) on ping-pong balls and put them in a small 'bedtime jar' so your child can feel some control over their routine as they independently pick out the balls one by one for a 'surprise' nighttime order of tasks or take them all out and decide what order to do them in themselves.

- If you are already locked in a head-to-head power struggle, put away your boxing gloves so your child will (eventually!) feel safe putting away theirs. When you battle with your child, you may win a skirmish or two, but you will lose the treasure...your trust relationship. Putting away the gloves means slowing down, breathing through your own emotions, and finding a way to work through the issue together. Remember, you're the adult in the relationship, but that doesn't give you the right to overpower your child; it gives you the responsibility to empower your child. That involves modeling the tools of diplomacy—

communication, cooperation, compromise—that you want your child to stock in their own emotional toolkit.

Remember, the children who come into the world with their 'boxing gloves on' so to speak are often the ones who become the biggest world changers. It's not easy raising these little world-changers, I know (*Believe me, I know. Two of my six are world-changers-in-the-making!*), but the rewards are phenomenal!

Chapter 17

You're Not the Boss of Me!

Few things ignite a parent's temper like defiance. It feels like a slap in the face, a direct challenge to our authority. Power card...played. Gauntlet...thrown. Challenge...accepted? Time out! No, not time-out as in punish your child, but time out as in hit the parental pause button, take a step back, assess the situation, and get some adult perspective.

There are three things to consider:

1. Behaviors are communication. What is your child trying to communicate?

2. Is the behavior really defiance, or did your child's action hit a nerve in you for some reason?

3. If the behavior is, in fact, defiance, what circumstances preceded it?

Once you've assessed the situation, you can more effectively address it. If your child is communicating an unmet need such as a need for more interaction from you, a need to be heard, or if they simply need an outlet for their energy, you can first meet those needs and then offer your child ideas about how to better communicate their needs to you in the future.

The same process applies if your child's behavior is communicating stress, anger, fear, or insecurity. Taking a step back allows you to not only see the emotion behind the action, but also gives you a moment to consider if there have been any big transitions in your child's life such as a move or change in childcare or a recent illness (or, possibly, a breach in trust if you have 'lost it' and yelled, threatened, or spanked) that they may have big feelings about but are not able to articulate. First, you can meet those emotional needs with empathetic listening, offering words to help them articulate their feelings, apologizing if you have broken trust with them, and helping them to process their pent up emotions. Then you can address their behavior by giving them options for expressing their needs in more acceptable ways.

Meeting their needs before addressing their behavior is vital because it lowers their defenses, clears whatever is cluttering up your parent/child connection, and opens the pathway to communication, in effect turning on their listening ears!

If in taking a step back to assess the situation you discover that your child's behavior isn't really defiance, but instead a nerve was hit in you that caused you to perceive it that way, you can first address your child's need and then their behavior, if necessary, but then take the time to address your own needs. Perhaps you have an unmet need to be heard by your spouse, boss, or even your own parents, or maybe there is a wound from your past that needs to be healed or a source of stress in your life that is causing you to feel overwhelmed. Taking an honest look at your own needs and hurts and stressors and dealing with those issues will not only benefit your parenting, but your life in general!

If your 'adult time-out' assessment reveals that the circumstances preceding your child's defiance contributed to it, you can learn from that and find ways to avoid those circumstances in the future. For instance, you may realize that hunger or tiredness or over-scheduling are triggers for your child's behavior. Or you may see that your wording is provoking a negative response. The word 'no' can be a trigger for a power struggle. Try rephrasing your no's into yes's. For example, instead of "No, you can't have ice cream until after dinner" you could try "I know you love ice cream. I do, too! We're getting ready to eat right now, but what flavor would you like after dinner?" The objective is to set the same limit, but phrase it in a way that invites cooperation instead of triggering opposition. You might realize you are inadvertently communicating your own stress to your child or even taking it out on them. Or you may have slipped into a negative parenting pattern and be 'powering up' on your child, in effect throwing down the gauntlet yourself, and they are merely reflecting your behavior. Whatever the case may be, learn from it, make the necessary adjustments, repair your relationship with an apology if needed, reconnect with your child, and then brainstorm ideas with your child about better ways both of you can handle things in the future.

Keep in mind, though, that sometimes what parents perceive as defiance is really just a child testing their boundaries to make sure that they are secure. Children need to know they're safe, and a parent who is confident and comfortable enough in their leadership to calmly and gently guide their child to stay within their boundaries is very reassuring. The goal of gentle discipline, however, is not controlling children, but equipping them to control themselves (In other words, we want to teach them to be 'the boss' of themselves!). So if your child is testing their boundaries, be careful to respond with guidance, not punishment.

Finally, remember, you are raising a little human with thoughts, needs, ideas, and a personality all their own. They aren't perfect any more than you are, and expecting perfection will lead to conflict, not connection. When they make mistakes, choose understanding, not anger. When they make poor choices, choose guidance, not punishment. And when they challenge your authority and throw down that gauntlet of defiance, choose peace, not warfare. Remember, you don't have to attend every fight you're invited to!

Chapter 18

A Place for Me

As a child, I loved to find a little 'hidey-hole' and tuck myself away from the big, wide world for a while. Somehow, sitting in a closet quietly singing to a much-loved babydoll, hiding in the leafy bower of an old grandfather oak with my nose in a book, or throwing a blanket over an end-table and crawling under it with a flashlight just made the world a little smaller, a little friendlier, a little less overwhelming. I remember feeling safe. I remember listening to the sound of my breathing, just listening. I remember closing my eyes and daydreaming, the cadence of my breath the only sound in the stillness.

It was there in the stillness, in the wanderings of my imagination, that I processed the brokenness of a broken home, adapted to the subsequent juggling of two homes, coped with the eventual abandonment by a father, and, over time, unlocked my guarded heart to a new father. It was in the smallness, in the microcosm of my own creation, that the big world shrunk down and the chaos receded and life's mountains became surmountable molehills.

With my own children, I've fallen in love anew with the 'hidey-hole.' Whether it's a fort of sofa cushions, a sheet with the ends tied to dining room chairs, a blanket hung over a coffee table, or the tree house built by my amazing husband, my children's imaginations take flight. And, as they make clubhouse signs and set about 'nesting' in their little corner of the world, their muffled giggles and busy chatter make my heart sing.

One parental adaptation I've made is called our Cozy Cave. It's a tucked-away spot with pillows and books and stuffed animals and a bit of privacy for a child to escape to when life feels a bit overwhelming or they notice their emotions are heading for a meltdown or their siblings are just a bit too much to take and they need a break.

It's not a place for punishments. It's not a place for them to be sent to take a break or think about what they've done. We do those things together so that I can be present and supportive and help them to process their big emotions.

Instead, our Cozy Cave is an open invitation to seek solace, to find some peace and quiet when *they* decide they need it, not when I decide they need it. They can read a book, shake a Calm-Me-Jar, cuddle some stuffed friends, or just sit in a small space and let their emotions drift down into a more manageable size. The Cozy Cave is the physical representation of an adult recognizing their need to step away from stress and mess and chaos and get some perspective. It is a place for children who are in the very beginning stages of learning self-regulation skills to practice those skills at their own pace.

I pray that the big, wide world out there is kind to my children, that they never know sadness, never taste bitterness, never experience disillusionment. But I know better. I know life can and will challenge and even hurt them. I know people will disappoint and hearts will be broken and dreams will be shattered.

But I also know the whispered comfort of familiarity and the value of a place of peace to process and to heal. I know that in the simplicity of play, the complexity of life can be sorted like puzzle pieces joined together to make sense of the world. And I know that in the nooks and niches we carve out for ourselves even as adults, the world seems a little smaller, a little friendlier, and a little less overwhelming.

Chapter 19

When Children Act Out:
Reflecting Our Emotions

Your sweet little four-year-old has suddenly started throwing his food at the table every. single. night. You've tried giving him smaller portions of food, letting him help plan the meals, letting him help cook the meals. You've tried asking him to stop, demanding that he stop, pleading with him to stop. You've tried rewards, sticker charts, and offering desserts. You've put him in time-out, yelled at him, even threatened to spank him, which you've never, ever done before. But still he throws food at the table.

Then it happens. You're sitting down for dinner and ask your spouse how the job hunt went that day. A little motion catches your eye and you glance at your four-year-old just in time to see a meatball fly across the table from a small, sauce-covered hand. But something else catches your attention, too, and instead of focusing on the flying meatball, this time you focus on your child.

In the split second before your little guy launched his food volley, you'd seen the fear, almost panic, in his eyes. Your mind races. Why, if he was so afraid of being spanked, would he go right ahead and throw his food? What in the world would make him do the very thing that might bring about the terrible consequence he seemed to be in a panic over?

You hear a deep sigh from your other side. Your spouse seems to be trying to control his urge to retaliate against the little food-fighter across the table from him. Teeth gritted tightly, he grabs a napkin, scoops up the meatball next to his plate, and resumes the conversation.

"Nothing. No one's hiring. I don't know what we're going to do."

Before you get a chance to respond, a meatball whizzes past your ear and lands smack in the middle of your husband's plate, splashing marinara sauce all over his shirt. He comes out of his seat with a roar and glares at the little guy who is glaring right back at him, now seemingly unafraid, almost taunting his father to make the next move.

But this time your husband sees something different. He sees the little quivering chin and the small clenched hands and realizes something else is going on. Quietly, he rounds the table and scoops his little fighter into a tight hug, irrespective of the marinara now coating both of their shirts. He doesn't say a word, just sinks into the chair with his son wrapped in his arms and holds him close against his heart.

As you see your angry, defiant son suddenly melt into his father and bury his face in his daddy's neck with body-wracking sobs, your own anger melts away. Soon, a small, tear-stained face peeks out and your heart breaks when your son looks back and forth between you and your husband, and his little voice croaks out, "What are we gonna do? Where will we live? Are we gonna starve?" before dissolving in sobs against his daddy's chest again.

That's when you realize dinner conversations have revolved around your husband's job loss and job search for months. Conversations from the past weeks run through your head, and you remember discussing getting a job outside the home to supplement the income from your own home-based business and putting your son into daycare. You remember your husband talking about selling your house, about where you would move, about saving on groceries and other bills. You cringe as you recall mentioning a friend who lost everything, including his home and marriage, when he lost his job.

What had your little preschooler been thinking all this time? What terror must he have felt imagining losing his home, not having enough food to eat, and even his mommy and daddy divorcing? The panic you'd seen in his eyes suddenly made all-too-much sense. He had no way of articulating his fears, the fears he'd felt and heard from you and your husband, but that neither of you had thought to discuss directly with him so that you could offer reassurance and comfort and answer his questions.

You're so, so thankful that you hadn't gone as far as actually hitting your son for the first time ever in an attempt to control him, and you vow to yourself that you will never threaten or try to coerce or manipulate your child again, just as you wouldn't your husband. You commit to finding better ways to communicate with your son, to remain in-tune with him, to focus on the need behind the behavior instead of just trying to control the behavior, to connect with him, and to equip him with better ways of communicating his needs.

As your husband looks up, his eyes wet with tears and his little man still clasped close to his heart, you meet his gaze and see the same realization, the same commitment, the same resolve. Life will still throw you curveballs, but from here on out you'll handle them together, all together.

Not every action by our children is a sign of trauma or deep, unresolved issues. But every behavior *is* communication. Behaviors can communicate simple needs such as hunger or the need for sleep. They can communicate unmet needs such as the need to be heard or the need to reconnect. They can communicate stress or discomfort over changes in routine or sickness. Or they can communicate big emotions our children need help processing.

But they can also be a reflection of and a reaction to *our* big emotions, our illnesses, our unmet needs, our stresses and anxieties, our emotional baggage. Just as children learn best by imitation, making it important to always be aware of the examples we set, in the same way their tendency to tune-in to our emotions and upsets makes it vital for us to stay in-tune with them so that we can alleviate their anxieties and answer their questions and ease their fears.

It's important to be open with them in age-appropriate language about ongoing family issues or health problems or other stresses, but remember that children are not equipped to handle adult stresses and emotions, so be careful to avoid dumping your emotional baggage on them in the process.

Simply reacting to our children's behavior rather than responding to the need motivating the behavior not only leaves us in the dark as to what our children are thinking and feeling, but also misses an opportunity to address the root of the behavior. When we pause, breathe through our own visceral reactions, and focus on our child instead of our child's actions, we can better discern the need behind the behavior and meet that need, thus eliminating the behavior itself with no need for correction and opening the door to guiding our children to better ways of expressing themselves in the future. The end result is not only the resolution of the present issue, but also the strengthening of the parent/child relationship which gives our children the reassurance that they aren't alone in dealing with their stresses and questions and fears and can always come to us, their 'safe haven' in times of need.

Chapter 20

For Everything There is a Season and a Time for Everything

Many parents misinterpret normal, childlike behaviors as unwanted intruders, weeds to be plucked, poisoned, and prevented so their little ones can flourish in the hothouse of childhood. What they don't realize is that childhood isn't a hothouse to be fenced in and closed off and climate-controlled. It's a wide-open, sun-drenched, wind-swept field of endless possibilities, experiences, and discoveries. And normal, childlike behaviors are the tumult of brilliant wildflowers sharing their vivid beauty in the riotous yellows of children shrieking and running in the sunshine, the gorgeous blues of children splashing in the sea, the stunning oranges of eyes lighting up in discovery, and the lovely purples of laughter floating on an afternoon breeze. They linger for an all-too-brief season before they're gone forever, lost in the business and busyness of adulthood.

This focus on weeding out normal behaviors seems ingrained in our modern rush-through-life mentality which has parents racing to correct behaviors and to push their children to reach developmental milestones and to force early independence. The thing is, though, that given time, independence will grow naturally on its own. Developmental milestones will be reached in a child's own unique timetable. Communication through behavior will evolve into verbal communication in its time.

Imagine how much conflict could be eliminated if we simply connected with our children where they are rather than pushing them to be where they aren't, if we listened with our hearts, provided guidance and understanding, modeled desired behaviors, and offered help when our children struggled.

Imagine how much more we, as parents, could enjoy our children's childhood if we took the time to see the world anew through our children's eyes, to appreciate the beauty inherent in the small moments of life, and to find our own childlike joy renewed as we discover again the ability to wonder as we revisit our own childhood to learn new truths about life, about ourselves, about the world.

Imagine those most precious gifts of parenting that we miss in our rush through life, those breathtaking moments of extraordinary joy a child finds in the most ordinary discoveries that can never be recaptured—the priceless first taste of a strawberry, the wonder of a butterfly's wings, the giggle at a kitten's batting paws, the belly laugh at a playmate's silly joke, the pride of a first bicycle ride, the excitement of a home run, the awe of a first loose tooth.

These are gifts our children long to share with us...if we'll only take the time to slow down and join them in the timeless, but oh-so-brief, moments of childhood.

Instead, though, we often methodically, albeit unknowingly, deny our children a childhood with our pushing and rushing and unreasonable expectations, and then we wonder why we have so many behavior issues with them. Even if our discipline approach is gentle, if we aren't letting our children be children, then we are missing the heart of gentle parenting entirely. Knowing our children, staying in-tune with their needs, nurturing their uniqueness, growing them into who they were created to be instead of molding them into who we want them to be, those are the tenets of gentle, respectful, responsive parenting.

Our children are children for such a small season of life. Let their laughter ring out, their imaginations soar, their feet stomp in puddles, their hands clap for joy. Too soon they will grow up and out of their youthful exuberance and zest and settle into the life and routine of adulthood. Don't make them settle too soon.

Chapter 21

Thoughtful Cooperation vs. Thoughtless Compliance

Someone once wrote, "Obedience is doing what you're told, no matter what's right. Morality is doing what's right, no matter what you're told." History preserved the quote, but not the source with any credibility, but it's a wise statement nonetheless.

Growing children with an inner compass that guides their steps toward kindness and compassion and generosity of spirit is far, far and away superior to training children to operate on automatic pilot. Parents often focus so much time and energy on trying to make their children obey in the small moments of life that they forget to step back and take a panoramic view of how their parenting choices may affect their children's life course.

"Instant obedience" is the new catch-phrase in many popular parenting articles and books, but the reality is that, while instant obedience may be convenient for parents in the moment, it can have powerful negative impacts on the adults their children will become. Training children into instant obedience is the equivalent of disabling their inner guidance system and strapping on a remote-controlled rocket. The end result may be adults who are easily controlled by others or adults who are deeply divided, constantly fighting the external controls, but hampered by an erratic, immature inner compass that never had the chance to develop properly.

Equipping children with a healthy, well-functioning internal guidance system, an inner compass, takes time, patience, and self-control on the part of the parents. Certainly not a convenient alternative! But, remember, convenience isn't one of the Three C's of gentle parenting. *Connecting, Communicating,* and *Cooperating* are the keys to gently guiding and growing our children into healthy adults. While it may not be convenient to slow down our hectic life pace and really connect with our children, it's that connection that enables their internal guidance system to come online. While taking the time to really communicate may be a sacrifice, it's in that communication that the directions on their inner guidance system are set. And, while working cooperatively with our children may take more time and effort, the fact is that inviting cooperation rather than forcing compliance raises leaders instead of reaping followers.

Clearly, teaching our children to control themselves is far more effective in the long-term than trying to control our children, but how, specifically, can we go about equipping them with those all-important internal controls?

- Model instead of manipulate.

- Invite instead of intimidate.

- Support instead of shame.

- Encourage instead of enrage.

- Teach instead of threaten.

- Listen instead of lecture.

- Help instead of hurt.

- Parent instead of punish.

Instant obedience and mindless compliance are poor goals, indeed, when raising children. A thoughtfully questioning, passionately curious, and humorously resourceful child who delights in inventing 'compromises' and who endlessly pushes the boundaries tends to become a thoughtful, passionate, resourceful adult who will change the world rather than being changed by the world.

Chapter 22

The Butterfly Effect

In the 2004 movie, *The Butterfly Effect,* twenty-year-old Evan (Ashton Kutcher) goes back in time to try to change events from his traumatic childhood in an attempt to change his dysfunctional adulthood. The movie's title is based on a mathematical prediction concept in chaos theory.

> *"In chaos theory, the butterfly effect is the sensitive dependence on initial conditions, where a small change at one place in a nonlinear system can result in large differences to a later state. The phrase refers to the idea that a butterfly's wings might create tiny changes in the atmosphere that may ultimately alter the path of a tornado or delay, accelerate, or even prevent the occurrence of a tornado in another location. The flapping wing represents a small change in the initial condition of the system, which causes a chain of events leading to large-scale alterations of events. Had the butterfly not flapped its wings, the trajectory of the system might have been vastly different."[13]*

So what does chaos theory have to do with parenting? Besides the obvious connection between chaos and parenting, it's about understanding the concept of "sensitive dependence on initial conditions," in other words, the power of early parenting choices to affect a child's future.

It is a well-documented fact that early childhood experiences powerfully influence later adulthood.[10] A childhood marred by abuse, violence, and trauma has profound implications in adulthood from continued cycles of abuse, to depression and other mental illnesses, to relational and life-satisfaction issues, and the negative effects are often far-reaching and destructive.

Not so well-documented is how the smaller differences in 'initial conditions,' or early parenting choices, can have significantly divergent outcomes. In these cases, it isn't abusive or neglect-filled childhoods versus normal childhoods that create the different outcomes, but instead more subtle differences in parenting that may have differing and often unforeseen long-term effects.

One family may breastfeed, another formula-feed. One family may bed-share, another room-share, while another sleeps entirely separately. One family may homeschool, another chooses private school, while another chooses a public education. One family may discipline (guide, teach, model, etc.) through connection, another may focus on behavior modification through negative or positive reinforcement, while another may rely heavily on punitive behavioral controls. Each parenting choice is a different 'initial condition' which can affect the overall trajectory of a child's life in powerful ways with the resulting outcome of adult behavior, relationships, career choices, etc. varying widely.

The goal of parenting, of course, cannot be perfection because we are imperfect people raising imperfect people in an imperfect world. So, while being aware of the significance of our decisions and making wise, educated choices is important, it is just as important to expect and account for parental missteps. Our mistakes can, in fact, become a vital part of raising our children to be gracious, forgiving adults. If we model taking personal responsibility for our mistakes along with forgiving ourselves, then our missteps can become virtual 'butterflies' on the slope into adulthood, redirecting the trajectory of our children's lives in a positive direction.

The redirective effect of the 'butterfly' on the slope into adulthood can also be called the redemptive effect. If we find that our parental choices are producing results in our children that we are unhappy with, we can redirect by setting in motion a butterfly's wings. In other words, we can shift our parenting style and reroute the trajectory of our children's lives.

Here are a few illustrations of The Butterfly Effect as it applies to parenting redirections...

A young girl with dyslexia comes home from school day after day in tears, exhausted and overwhelmed, only to have to spend hours at night struggling through homework, more tears, and then get up the next day to do it all over again. Her father realizes that with his daughter's unique learning style, traditional schooling is like teaching a butterfly to swim, with the result that his little butterfly's wings would be forever damaged and she'd never learn to fly. He turns his life upside down to make the time to homeschool her and find ways to emphasize her strengths and turn her weaknesses into gifts. His daughter transforms from a withdrawn child with low self-worth into a confident young lady soaring into a bright future.

~~~~~~~

A young mother brings home a precious newborn she loves with every fiber of her being. She wants the absolute best for her child and has read book after book saying that proper training of a child has to start right from the beginning. It hurts her all the way down to her soul as each night she gently and lovingly tucks her sweet baby into his crib and walks away, closing the door on his cries and sliding down onto her knees in the hallway to spend night after sleepless night crying right along with him. After the first torturous nights, she finds that her baby isn't nursing well on the strict schedule the books suggested, and her milk supply hadn't come in as expected. The pediatrician diagnoses failure-to-thrive and suggests supplementing with formula. As the young mother leaves the doctor's office in tears, feeling like her body has failed her, an older mother sees her distress and approaches her in the parking lot. When the young mother pours out her story, the older mother shares her own struggles and discoveries over the years, ending by encouraging the young mother to bring her baby into her room at night and nurse him on demand to see if her milk supply increases. The young mother is relieved to hear there are alternatives to the rigid training methods she'd read about. She takes the older mother's advice and over the next days and night discovers that not only does her milk supply increase substantially, but both she and her new baby are finally getting some sleep! She tosses the baby training idea out the window and spreads her parenting wings, parenting from the heart, making every parenting decision by first asking herself how she would want someone to respond to her if she were the child. Her son grows up strong and healthy, with a deep respect and empathy for others.

~~~~~~~

A father is struggling with his three-year-old's temper. He has poured himself into raising his daughter 'right' from birth, reading her stories every night, feeding her nutritious foods, getting her into the best preschool, correcting her with carefully controlled spankings dealt in love and followed by hugs and kisses. As he heads to pick up his daughter from preschool, his stomach tightens in dread. For the second time that week they've called him to report another incidence of aggressive behavior by his daughter, and he knows when they get home he'll have to punish her. He sighs in discouragement. She used to be such a sweet, bubbly little girl. Now she just seems to simmer, anger hovering just beneath the surface ready to burst out at the slightest provocation. He heads into the preschool and signs his daughter out, then reaches out to help her into her coat. She flinches at his touch and flings her tiny hands up instinctively to protect herself. For one moment, their eyes meet, and the father's heart freezes. Fear. Ever so briefly, instead of that too-familiar anger clouding his little girl's eyes, fear had stared back at him. Feeling sick, the father gently helps his daughter

into her coat and picks her up, hiding his tears by
hugging her close as he walks to the car. Never again,
he vows. Never again will his precious daughter look at
him in fear. At home, he sits his daughter down and
tells her that he's sorry, that hands are for helping, not
hitting, and that they're going to work together to find
better ways to handle things when people don't do what
they want. His daughter's anger eases over time and
trust returns. She grows into a compassionate young
woman, serving her community with a gentle passion
that wins hearts everywhere she goes.

In each case, the parent was faced with the reality that the track their parenting choices had placed their child on wasn't optimal, and each parent responded by shifting course and altering the trajectory of their child's life, in turn altering their child's future in immeasurable ways.

The message here is this ~ our parenting choices *matter*. They matter in life-defining ways that we can't even imagine when we wrap those precious new lives in the cocoon of our love and set them on a path which we hope and pray will help them to spread their wings and fly. Choose wisely, parents, and don't be afraid to change course in mid-flight if the winds are blowing in the wrong direction.

Chapter 23

The Color of Change

So few parents today were raised peacefully and respectfully by their own parents that it's no surprise that a big issue in the gentle parenting community is how to overcome the stumbling blocks of change. Moving from a control-based parenting style, whether you're used to spanking or time-outs or reward charts or some combination of the three, to a connection-based parenting style is a heart and mindset change as much as it is a lifestyle change. The undeniable fact is that change is hard work. Whether you're trying to overcome your own childhood or your own already-established parenting habits, you can expect it to get harder before it gets easier. Just like with any lifestyle change, you will hit walls along the way, and they might even knock you back a step or two. Here are five tips to help you keep calm and carry on to achieve your parenting goals:

1. Commit to no hitting or other physical expressions of anger or frustration, and let that be your starting point, the line in the sand that you absolutely will not cross. Just like in marriage, if you don't make a commitment, there's nothing to keep you from straying back into old patterns.

2. Rethink your parenting role and move away from trying to force or manipulate or plead or coerce or use any other tactic to try to control your child's behavior and instead build a desire in your child to cooperate because they trust you to make good decisions and to want them to be happy and safe. Do that by taking all of that energy that's been going into trying to control their behavior (external controls) and focusing it on trying to build your connection and modeling the behavior you want to encourage (building internal controls).

3. Examine what you're modeling. If right now you are insisting on your own way and reacting emotionally with anger and power-plays to your child's lack of cooperation, what are you modeling? Stubbornness and lack of emotional regulation (i.e. adult-style tantrums). If, instead, you connect with your child, engage them in creative problem-solving, and work together with them toward a resolution to whatever issue you're having, what are you modeling? Compromise, resourcefulness, and cooperation. Definitely worthwhile life lessons!

4. Keep working on *you*. Remind yourself that it's *your* emotions and experiences and expectations that are causing your outbursts, not your little one's behavior. Ask yourself why you're so upset. Explore your inner triggers. Work through that internally instead of reacting to it externally. (See Chapter Fifteen for more about healing your own hurts.)

5. Choose a touchstone in a color that will help to keep you grounded, something to look at or hold on to when you feel yourself slipping back into old thinking and behavior patterns. It could be a necklace or bracelet or key chain in a color that captures the essence of the parent you want to be to help you stay focused as you work your way toward becoming that parent. Colors have psychological implications, so some good choices might be blue which is the color of peace and trust; turquoise which is the color of communication; pink which is the color of unconditional love; or magenta which is the color of harmony. You can also place the color around your house as a reminder of the peaceful home you're trying to create and as a symbol of change and renewal to help you remember to stop and breathe and think *before* responding to your child.

Remember, it's a huge change to go from demanding obedience to inviting cooperation, and if you are already in an adversarial pattern with your child, that process will take extra time and patience. And keep in mind that no parenting 'works' to change a child into an adult or into a perfect little puppet. Children are children, as they should be. But shifting your thinking from expecting, or demanding, obedience to working with your child, understanding them, connecting with them, and inviting them to cooperate (i.e. Instead of "If you don't put your dinner dishes in the sink, you won't get ice cream for dessert" try "Let me know when your dishes are in the sink so I can get your ice cream for you.") is the first and most important step toward a gentler style of parenting and a more peaceful home.

Chapter 24

Bridge Over Troubled Water:
Parenting a 'Problem' Child

We all have times when we struggle, when life gets hard, when stresses overtake us and the constant demands to grow and change and learn inherent in simply being human just feel like too much to bear.

Children are no different than adults in that they, too, can often feel overwhelmed by life. The sheer volume of growth and change and learning integral to childhood inevitably produce stress, though that isn't necessarily a negative for all children. Some children, just like some adults, seem to have an innate ability to cope with stress, to adapt to change, and to face and conquer challenges. Some personalities even thrive on it!

But then there are those children who simply seem to struggle with life. Growth spurts cause incredible stress and discomfort. Change produces intense anxiety and resistance. And learning, being introduced to new thoughts and ideas, being stretched and challenged, inspires unease and distress.

These children are often labeled problem children, strong-willed, difficult, entitled, or brats. The reality, though, is that these are often the most sensitive children, small people who were created to be intimately in-tune with their bodies, their environment, and their fellow human beings. They feel, deeply and empathetically, other people's pain and distress. They endure shifts in their surroundings like frontal assaults to their safety and security. They experience touch and movement of their bodies, and growth within their bodies, with painful intensity.

All too often, these sensationally gifted children are misunderstood. Their strong reactions to stimuli are misinterpreted as willfulness and stubbornness. They are punished instead of helped, controlled instead of supported, hurt instead of heard. Their uniqueness, gifts, and insights are forced underground where they often simmer in silence, bursting forth in flashes of rage or turning inward in brooding depression.

These children don't need labels. They don't need to be contained or controlled. They need what all children need…love, understanding, and guidance to grow into the gifted, unique individuals they were created to be.

Helping and supporting your sensitive child who is struggling is like building a bridge over troubled waters using the Three C's of gentle discipline:

Connect:

1. Observe and really get to know, understand, and appreciate the gifts and needs of the unique little person you are privileged to parent.

2. Build a foundation of trust and respect in your parent/child relationship by 'listening' to the needs being expressed by your child's behavior even when their behavior seems completely out of proportion to the situation.

Communicate:

3. Keep an open door policy, particularly in the late evening hours when the house is quiet and everyone else is settled for the night. Sensitive children often need stillness to feel safe enough to begin processing all of the overwhelming stimuli and emotions they experience throughout the day.

4. Help them to verbalize their feelings and experiences by listening to their hearts and not just their words, and quietly offering observations to help them to put things into perspective.

Cooperate:

5. Work with your sensitive child to help them find coping mechanisms that will help them deal with overwhelming sensations, emotions, and situations. Some ideas are to offer them options such as...

    •   wearing noise-cancelling headphones to block out extraneous noises

    •   escaping to a Cozy Cave to take a break from the stresses of daily life (see Chapter Eighteen)

    •   creating a private code word that they can use to let you know they are feeling overwhelmed or that you can use to alert them that they may need to take a break or to dial things down a notch or two

6. Equip them with tools to express themselves in acceptable ways (i.e. "It's not okay to be rude, but it is okay to tell someone you need a break" or "It's not okay to run away at school, but it is okay to go to your teacher and tell them you're having a hard time.")

7. Work with them intentionally on a daily basis to overcome the stresses and minimize the impacts of what is, to us, normal daily life, but to them can be deeply troubling experiences.

Building a strong, supportive bridge into the future with your sensitive child will provide them with the coping skills they'll need as adults to overcome normal stresses and challenges as well as those that come when life inevitably flows into troubled and turbulent waters.

Chapter 25

Raising Problem Solvers

"Discipline is helping a child solve a problem. Punishment is making a child suffer retribution for having a problem. To raise problem solvers, focus on solutions, not retributions."

When children act out negatively, they are communicating that they are experiencing a problem they aren't able to solve on their own. With very young children the problem tends to be unmet needs such as hunger, attention, comfort, understanding, etc. or frustrations such as not being able to do things themselves or not being able to communicate what they want verbally. With older children, however, the problems are often more external such as issues with friends or siblings or problems with teachers or schoolwork pressures.

While the behavior itself may seem to be the problem to parents, it is actually merely a symptom of a deeper problem that the child needs help working through. Focusing on the symptom, the behavior, doesn't address the cause of that behavior, leaving children to struggle alone without guidance and almost ensuring that the negative behavior will resurface.

When it comes to 'problem behaviors' there are four types of parents…parents who punish their children for having problems, parents who view their children as being problems, parents who solve their children's problems for them, and parents who help their children solve their problems.

All behavior, though, both positive and negative, is communication, so if a parent's focus is simply on stopping their child's behavior, the parent is, in effect, silencing their child.

- If a parent punishes their child for having a problem, the problem goes unsolved and the child learns no problem-solving skills. What the child does learn, though, is not to trust their parent with their problems.

- If a parent gives their child whatever they want because they just want the behavior to stop or if a parent offers bribes to get the behavior to stop, the parent is, in effect, still silencing their child. The problem still goes unsolved, and the child learns no problem-solving skills. What the child does learn, though, is that negative behaviors may be rewarded.
- If a parent solves the problem for their child, the problem may get solved, but the child still learns no problem-solving skills.

In no way do any of these parental responses grow problem solvers or healthy adults.

The fourth type of parent, though, responds to their child's problem behaviors by partnering with their child to help them solve the problem prompting the behavior, thus resolving the behavior issue, teaching problem-solving skills that their child can take into the future, and preserving and building on the parent/child trust foundation, a vital connection to maintain throughout the teen years and into adulthood.

Teaching and modeling problem solving-skills may sound a bit complicated, but in actuality it's what you've already been practicing if you've been using the Three C's of gentle discipline—intentional connection, open communication, and inviting cooperation—in your home.

To break it down even further, though, here's a simple illustration:

> Do you remember learning about simple machines in school? You know, the inclined plane (to roll things up and down on), the pulley (to raise and lower things), the screw (to hold things together), etc. Simple machines

are designed to make difficult tasks a bit...well, simpler! One simple machine that makes lifting heavy loads a bit easier is a lever. So, parents, here are your L.E.V.E.R.S. to help your children when their load gets a bit too heavy for them to bear alone and they need some guidance through the problem-solving process.

Listen

Empathize

Validate

Evaluate

Reiterate

Support

1. *Listen* not only to your child's words, but also to their behavior, and look for the need they are communicating.

2. *Empathize* with the emotion you perceive your child is struggling with. For instance, you may say something like, "I can hear how upset you are."

3. *Validate* the difficulty your child is experiencing. For example, "It is hard when people aren't kind" or "That is a tough thing to deal with."

4. *Evaluate* potential solutions with your child by asking questions to clarify the problem and to get them thinking about possible answers, reflecting back what you're hearing from them, and offering suggestions of your own if they ask for them.

5. *Reiterate* the problem, potential solutions, and your confidence in their ability to handle problems on their own, as well as your availability to help them if they need you.

6. *Support* their attempts to work through their problem by remaining in-tune with their efforts, helping them to process their emotions, and being ready to step in with assistance if you see that they are getting overwhelmed.

Always keep in mind, though, that while the goal is to equip your children with the skills they need to solve problems on their own when they are adults, until then you are the adult they are relying on.

Chapter 26

Children of Violence

A child of a long-time broken home recently went to live with his father for the first time. Up until that point, he'd lived with his mother and visited his father every other weekend for most of his life.

A few weeks after moving in with his father, the young teen found himself desperately barricaded in his room with his beer-guzzling, pot-bellied, enraged father kicking down his door. His father burst through the door and attacked him, pinning him against the wall, hitting him over and over again.

The boy tried to block the blows. He pushed his way past his father to try to get out of the room, but was caught and flung back into the room and hit repeatedly.

A neighbor called the police... who subsequently arrested the child for assaulting his father. The young teen was not even allowed to give a statement to the police.

In the back of the squad car on the way to Juvenile Detention for the first time in his life, the sobbing boy asked, "What was I supposed to do when my father attacked me?"

The arresting officer replied, "Nothing. Your father has a right to physically punish you as long as he doesn't do any significant damage." The officer glanced in the rearview mirror. "And I don't see any significant damage. You don't have the right to defend yourself."

The young teen asked, "Can I run away?"

The officer said, "You can try. Maybe a neighbor will help you. But don't call us or we'll just take you back to your father. He's within his rights. We can't help you."

This is a true story. It happened just a few weeks ago. Unfortunately, it's not an isolated story, by any means.

In the United States it is legal for a parent to hit a child. It is illegal for a child to hit a parent.

It is legal in nineteen states for a school official to hit a child. It is illegal for a child to hit a school official. Children as young as six have been arrested and placed in handcuffs for assaulting school officials.[14]

Children, the smallest and most vulnerable of Americans, are the only citizens of the US who have no rights, no voice. They can't vote. They can't defend themselves. They can't leave. They can't file assault charges. But they can be charged with assault.

When are we as a nation going to realize that the way we treat children is the way they will treat others? How long will we continue to train our children in our homes and schools that 'might is right' but then act shocked and dismayed when they take that lesson onto playgrounds and into classrooms in the form of bullying those smaller and more vulnerable than themselves? How many more anti-bullying campaigns will be tried and fail because they focus on controlling children's behavior instead of addressing the causes of that behavior? At what point will the truth that violence breeds violence penetrate the minds and hearts of mainstream America so that real and lasting change will finally become possible?

What message will the young teen, assaulted by his own father, arrested for defending himself, and told that authorities could not and would not protect him, take into the future? What kind of an adult will he become? What kind of world will these children of violence and trained helplessness create for all of us when they become the next world leaders? Do you see peace in our future?

There is another way. We can live what we want our children to learn. We can be the adults we want them to become. We can show them compassion, respect, and understanding so that we sow kindness, peace, and empathy in their hearts. We can stop bullying before it starts by not bullying our own children.

There is great truth to the old adage, "Hurting people hurt people." Let's stop raising our children by hurting them and start raising our children by loving them, instead.

Chapter 27

The Discipline of Choice

Many parents believe that adolescence is synonymous with rebellion. They believe that negative attitudes and backtalk and arguments and sneaking out at night and a myriad of other behavior issues are inevitable results of the suffix –*teen* becoming attached to their child's age. But the reality is that rebellion is not inevitable. When a child has nothing to rebel against, they don't feel the need to rebel. And when a child has been raised with respect, acceptance, and kindness, those attributes become as deeply entrenched in their heart as hurt and anger become entrenched in the heart of a child who was shamed, threatened, and intimidated to control their behavior in early childhood.

That does not mean, however, that teens raised with connection, communication, and cooperation will be perfect. They are still human, and they are still children. A teen who was gifted with a strong will as a young child will still be gifted with a strong will as a teen child. A teen who struggled with sensory issues as a young child will still be learning to cope with those issues as a teen child. And all teens, even those who are very articulate, will struggle to put their big adolescent emotions into words.

In other words, the teen years are not the time to stop viewing behavior as communication. In fact, just the opposite. When caught up in the big hormonal upheavals and concomitant emotional storms, most teens lose the ability to articulate, or even to understand, what they are feeling and why they are behaving as they are. Even in the teen years, behavior, both positive and negative, is communication, and a gentle parent can 'listen between the lines' for the need being communicated and work with their teen to help them process their feelings and guide them through the steps to find solutions to their problems. (see Chapter Twenty-Five)

One reason the adolescent years have such a bad reputation is that often during the middle childhood years there is a lull in the parenting challenges because children aren't coping with huge growth spurts or teething or struggling to learn to walk and talk and potty or going through any of the other huge transitions that spark most of the emotional meltdowns of toddlerhood. That lull can make the often sudden, marked increase in emotional ups and downs of the teen years seem like a beginning of the 'inevitable' rebellion of adolescence, and many parents will hurry to crack down on their children to try to nip the negative behaviors in the bud. Unfortunately, that reactionary response simply adds fuel to the very fires the parents are trying to proactively put out.

In actuality, though, the sudden increase in volatility isn't a sign of impending rebellion, but rather it is a sign of impending rapid growth—physically, mentally, and emotionally. That rapid growth is, in many ways, a return to the intense vulnerability and sensitivity of toddlerhood as teens grapple with big life changes, big emotions, and big hormonal shifts.

As such, parents who respond to their teens with the same compassion, the same empathy, the same supportive presence and gentle guidance that they employed with their toddlers will find that their connection to their teens remains healthy and their communication remains strong and the cooperative spirit they've created in their relationship remains intact.

That is not to say that there will be no troubles or trials or dramas or disagreements. Teens are human and they are children, and on both counts they will have their ups and downs and good days and bad days. But it does mean that the Three C's of gentle discipline—Connection, Communication, and Cooperation—are as valid and effective in the teen years as they are in the other stages of childhood. And it does mean that rebellion and attitudes and arguing are not inevitable results of the advent of the teen years.

The focus of discipline at this stage is twofold—parental discipline and circumstantial discipline. Parental discipline looks much the same as it did in the other stages of gentle parenting because the Three C's of gentle discipline—Connection, Communication, and Cooperation—naturally evolve with children's ever-changing needs by keeping parents in-tune and responsive to their children. They are summed up by the simple phrases, "I'm here. I hear you. How can I help?"

It is the circumstantial discipline that teens grapple with that comes powerfully into play at this stage, though, that marks the beginning of the end of parental discipline. It is the discipline of choice, of growing and learning through good decisions and bad, of learning through making mistakes, of learning to trust themselves by being trusted, of knowing that when they do fail they will be helped and healed and supported and not hurt and belittled and abandoned. It is the discipline of life as parents intentionally begin to let go, releasing their teens to try and fail and win and lose and get up the next morning to do it all again with the sure knowledge that they always have a safe harbor, a helping hand, a strong shoulder, and a loving heart waiting for them at home.

Chapter 28

Helping Hurting Teens

When children aren't parented in the early years with gentleness and respect, the teen years can hit the family with the force of a hurricane. Parents who have felt confident in their control over their children up until this point often find themselves lost, dazed, and bewildered, entangled in a parenting morass of their own making. The truths they discover shock them and leave them vulnerable and defenseless in the face of outright or passive mutiny:

1. Hitting doesn't lead to hugging. Just ask the mother struggling with her teenage daughter who had become withdrawn around the age of twelve or thirteen, often spending hours in her room and refusing to engage with the rest of the family. The mother recognized that there was a problem, but interpreted it as laziness, selfishness, and rebellion. The mother said, "She won't accept discipline given in love anymore, and I don't know how to control her behavior." The 'discipline given in love' turned out to be being spanked with a paddle wielded by a parent who then demanded an apology from the child for her behavior, followed by a hug. This mother discovered that, once her daughter reached her teen years, she no longer accepted the hitting, and she no longer accepted the hugs, either.

2. Lectures don't lead to learning. Just ask the father who complained that every time he sat his son down to read him the riot act for something, he could see his son's eyes glaze over as the teen retreated to an inner world. The father would repeatedly demand that his son pay attention, and his son would then quote his lecture

verbatim, but nothing worked to change his son's behavior. The father shared, "I don't know what to do. How can I control my son if I can't reach him?" What this father is discovering is that lecturing instead of listening is a one-way street that leads nowhere.

3. Coercion doesn't lead to cooperation. Just ask the mother who was so frustrated with her son's inability to finish his math homework that she began to take his things and hold them as ransom to try to force him to cooperate. She emptied his room piece by piece, day after day, until she'd literally taken away everything he owned, including every article of clothing except for the clothes on his back. After six weeks of her son wearing the same clothes and sleeping on the floor, she said, "I don't know what else I can take away from him. He doesn't have anything left! How can I control him now?" What this mother found was that you can't force cooperation and children outgrow coercion just like they outgrow clothing.

4. Ridicule doesn't lead to respect. Just ask the father who made his daughter post on Facebook that she had lied to her parents about her screen-time and couldn't be trusted to have a laptop, so she wouldn't be online for a month. The father was infuriated to then discover that his daughter was using friends' computers, so he made her call every one of her friends' parents and explain why she wouldn't be visiting for the next month. When the father found out his daughter was using the computers at the library, he made her stand in front of the library with a sign that said, "I'm a liar." A week later the father found his daughter online in the middle of the night, using a laptop borrowed from a friend. The father said, "What can I do? Every time I find a way to control my daughter, she finds a way around it. How can I make her respect me?" What this father is finding is that you can't force respect. Ridicule and shame are disrespectful and only breed more disrespect.

What these parents are discovering, and what you may have already discovered yourself as your children have reached adolescence, is that no matter how much you escalate punishments, they won't work to get your children under *your* control because one human can never really control another. Yes, you can overpower a small child, and you can use fear and intimidation and manipulation to force children to comply, but only for a season. Once they reach the teen years and their own identity begins to fully emerge, they gain enough separation to realize that they can finally say no to the hitting and threats and manipulations. They may say no with outright rebellion or by withdrawing into passive resistance, but they *will* say no, and then you are lost because you haven't built a relationship based on mutual respect and cooperation. You've simply spent years forcing your will on a smaller, weaker human.

Can you make changes, even this late in parenting? Yes. Stop hitting, threatening, intimidating, coercing, shaming, and trying to control your child. Wipe the slate clean with a sincere apology, and then start rebuilding your relationship from the ground up:

- Create a foundation of trust by proving *yourself* trustworthy. That means honoring your word that you won't punish or manipulate your teen to try to control them, no matter what.

- Sacrifice your own hopes and dreams for your teen and support their hopes and dreams. Will they make mistakes? Yes. That's part of life. Let them make the mistakes without repercussion from you, and help them through the natural results of those mistakes so they will know they can count on you when life hurts.

- Set limits *with* your teen instead of *for* your teen. Ask their opinion about curfews and relationships and housework. Tell them that it's an honor system from this point on, no punishments, and ask them how you can help them to honor the limits they've helped set.

- Remember that, while your teen is rapidly approaching adulthood, they are still a child and still need guidance. Don't disconnect (i.e. give up) and just let your teen figure things out for themselves. Yes, they do need to try and fail and try again so they can learn from their mistakes, but that doesn't mean they don't need you. Your role at this point is supportive as you stay in-tune and available and help them to process all of the big transitions and emotions and events that happen in adolescence. Walk them through the problem-solving steps (see Chapter Twenty-Five) as many times as they need you to so that they can learn how to become problem solvers themselves.

- If they backtalk, LISTEN (see Appendix B). If they struggle with homework, help them. If they lie, forgive them and work with them to come to a place where they feel safe to be truthful. If they break curfew, ask them why and work with them to sort out the problem.

- Memorize these words, "I'm here. I hear you. How can I help?" They encapsulate the Three C's of gentle parenting—Connection. Communication. Cooperation. Use them every day to rebuild your relationship.

The thing to remember is that you are the only adult in the relationship for the time being, so be the first one to listen, the first one to forgive, the first one to apologize, the first one to understand, the first one to back down and try to find another way when the going gets tough. Before you know it, your teen will be an adult, just like you… Just. Like. You. Make sure the 'you' they see is the 'you' that you want them to become.

Chapter 29

12 Life Lessons for Daughters

1. Your kisses are priceless. Don't give them away for free.

2. You are priceless. Treat yourself that way, and others will, too.

3. Don't let the world tell you whether you're beautiful or not. Live your beauty and let the world take notes.

4. Don't wait for opportunity. Make your own.

5. You matter. So does everyone else. Be fair. Be kind. Be honest.

6. There is nothing second best about being a female. Embrace every bit of your femininity. That's where your strength lies.

7. When life feels too big to handle, go outside. Everything looks smaller when you're standing under the sky.

8. A smile is the secret to true beauty. Smile at yourself when you look in the mirror and see how lovely you really are.

9. The best boyfriends are found in books, not in high school. Teenage boys aren't ready for love, and you're worth all the love in the world.

10. Sex is just sex without love.

11. Exercise and eat well to be healthy, not to change yourself.

12. If anyone ever tells you that you can't, prove them wrong.

Chapter 30

12 Life Lessons for Sons

1. Take showers. Comb your hair. Dress neatly. You never know when you're going to meet your future boss or coworker or wife or employee. First impressions matter.

2. Alcohol kills brain cells. Drink water and save the cells!

3. Being a man of honor isn't old-fashioned. Honor your word. Honor your friends. Honor your parents. Honor yourself.

4. Figure out where you want to go with your life sooner rather than later, then make a plan to get there. Destinations can always be changed, but you won't get anywhere in idle.

5. Girls are people. Get to know the person, not just the face.

6. Love is a choice, not a feeling. Until you understand that, you aren't ready for love.

7. Sex is just sex without love. If you're not ready for love, you're not ready for sex.

8. Work hard. It matters.

9. Exercise your brain, not just your biceps.

10. Obstacles are opportunities. Knock them down and get on with it.

11. Deodorant. Use it.

12. If you need help ask for it. If someone else needs help, give it. We're all in this together.

Appendix A

[From *Two Thousand Kisses a Day: Gentle Parenting Through the Ages and Stages*]

It's been said that it takes twenty-one days to make or break a habit and that change comes easiest and lasts longest when it's undertaken in small, bite-sized chunks. Those same principles apply when trying to transform your parenting, as well. Simply resolving on January 1st that, from that day forward, you are going to be a gentle parent and trying to change everything all at once is just setting yourself up for disappointment, frustration, and, more than likely, failure, followed by that age-old enemy of peace...mommy guilt.

Instead, try setting yourself up for success by taking a year of 'baby steps' to create real, lasting transformation in your parenting. Here are twelve steps you can start any time of the year, not just on January 1st, that offer practical, effective guidance to help you on your journey to gentle parenting. Keep in mind, though, that failure is a natural, normal part of change, so remember to give yourself grace when you fail. (Also, giving yourself grace is good practice for learning to extend that same grace to your children, which is a hallmark of gentle parenting!)

January (Step 1)

Slow down! ~ Gentle parenting is, at its core, based on a strong, healthy parent/child connection, so intentionally including time in your life to build and maintain that connection is vital. Start the year off by examining your daily and weekly schedule and looking for things to reduce or eliminate. Add up how much time your children spend in school, sleeping, in daycare, with babysitters, at sports practices, in music lessons, etc. and look at how much or little time is left over. Time for your family to connect, time to play, time to simply be, are just as important as those other activities, if not more so! Eliminate and reduce what you can, and look for ways to build connection into the things you can't eliminate. For instance, if your child has homework each night, why not sit down and work through the homework with them? As humans, we learn better through interaction, anyway, so you'll not only be connecting, you'll be enriching your child's education in the process! Another area that might benefit from a connection 'rehab' is that morning rush to get ready and out the door. Try getting everyone up a half hour earlier to ease the morning stresses that often lead to conflict and can result in a parent/child disconnect.

February (Step 2)

Listen! ~ Once you've slowed down enough to breathe, it's time to stretch yourself and grow as a parent. Like most changes in life, it won't come easy, but the rewards are well worth it. Fred Rogers said, "Listening is where love begins," meaning that when we listen, we really get to know someone, learn about what motivates them, and understand their thoughts, hopes, dreams, hurts, disappointments, etc. All behaviors communicate underlying needs, and what we learn about the inner life of our children by listening to them will help us to focus on the needs behind the behaviors instead of simply correcting the 'symptoms' (i.e. the behavior).

As a parent, it may seem instinctive to insist that our children listen to us so that our guidance and/or correction can be heard. In fact, the number one complaint I get from most parents is, "My children just don't listen!" to which I respond, "Do you?"

The reality is that if a child doesn't feel they are being heard, then even if they stand silently 'listening' while we lecture or rant or even just talk, the child is simply rehearsing in their brain what they want to say rather than actually doing any effective listening. As the only adults in the parent/child relationship, it's up to the parent to be the first to listen, to *really* listen, because we are the ones with the maturity and self-control to be able to patiently wait to be heard.

March (Step 3)

Live what you want them to learn! ~ Ralph Waldo Emerson said, "What you do speaks so loud that I cannot hear what you say." Consciously, intentionally, and consistently living out how you want your children to turn out is the most powerful and effective character training there is. If you want your children to be kind, be kind. If you want them to be respectful, respect them. If you want them to learn self-control, model self-control. If you want them to be compassionate, treat them with compassion. If you want them to feel joy, enjoy them. If you want them to feel valuable, treasure them. The bottom line is, your children are always watching and learning, so make sure what they see in you is what you want to see in them!

April (Step 4)

Breathe! ~ We all get overwhelmed by the seemingly endless demands of life at times, so this month remind yourself to relax and consciously focus on enjoying your children. It's just a fact of human nature that when we enjoy something, we pay more attention to it, value it, and treat it better. Applying that fact to parenting, it makes sense to be intentional about taking time to laugh and hug and simply be with our children. Check out the 'bucket list' in chapter 15 of *Two Thousand Kisses a Day: Gentle Parenting Through the Ages and Stages* full of ideas for simple, memorable fun to share with life's most precious treasures, your children!

May (Step 5)

Book it! ~ It's been said that our treasure lies where our time, attention, and love is invested. While having special family outings and activities is a wonderful way to enjoy our children, it is in the daily routines and busyness of life that the parent/child connection can often suffer the most. One of the best ways to stay connected with our children is to build time into each day to invest in them, and one of the best investments is in a love of reading. A love of reading is born on the lap of a parent, in the soothing cadence of a mother's voice reading the same beloved story night after night, in the rhythmic sway of a rocking chair, and in the comfortable rustle of well-worn pages being turned one after another after another. A quiet bedtime routine that includes a nighttime story will not only help bedtime to be happier and smoother, but will also incorporate vital time for you to reconnect with your children at the end of every day.

June (Step 6)

Turn your no's into yes's! ~ In any home, like in any civilized society, boundaries are necessary for everyone's safety and comfort. With gentle parenting, setting limits focuses on connection and empathetic communication rather than control and punitive consequences. This month try setting limits using gentle parenting by turning your *no's* into *yes's*. Instead of *"No, you can't have ice cream until after dinner,"* try *"I know you love ice cream. I do, too! We're getting ready to eat right now, but what flavor would you like after dinner?"* This invites cooperation instead of triggering opposition, another hallmark of gentle parenting.

July (Step 7)

Play! ~ They say that the family that plays together, stays together, and there's great truth to that. Play is the language of childhood, and through play we get to know and connect with our children on their turf, in their native language, and on their terms. It's a powerful moment in a parent's life when they suddenly see their sweet little one as a separate, intelligent, worthy human being who can plan, make decisions, snap out orders, and lead other humans on a journey through an imaginary rainforest or on a trip through outer space. This month, try taking on the role of follower in your child's land of make-believe, and you'll discover a whole new world in which your child is strong, confident, and capable, and you'll come away with a deeper connection with and appreciation for the *person*, not just the child.

August (Step 8)

Eat well! ~ Along with all of the exercise you'll be getting playing with your child, take stock of the kinds of food you're providing to fuel their little engines and enrich their minds. Good nutrition may not be the first thought that pops into people's minds when they think of gentle parenting, but studies have shown that many behavior issues and sleep problems have their root in unhealthy eating habits, nutrient-poor diets, and food additives (dyes, preservatives, etc.). Children, especially littler ones, don't take change well as a general rule, and changes to the foods they eat are on top of the list of changes they'll resist. As a gentle parent, working with, instead of against, our children will help to make eating healthy a fun family project instead of a food fight. Try letting your children help you make weekly menus and shop for the fresh ingredients you'll be using, and let them help you cook, too. If they feel like they are a part of the change instead of a victim of it, they're far more likely to cooperate. If you have picky eaters, don't hesitate to serve them the same foods you normally do, just with a few added healthy ingredients slipped in to make them healthier. (For ideas on ways to make healthy changes more fun, check out Chapter Nine of *Two Thousand Kisses a Day: Gentle Parenting Through the Ages and Stages*.)

September (Step 9)

Don't forget your funny bone! ~ Often the best parenting advice is simply, *"Chill out! Relax! Laugh a little, for goodness' sake!"* Sometimes as parents we get so caught up in 'fixing' our children that all we see are problems. We start focusing so much on preparing our children for their future that we forget to let them live in the present. One of the main problems with that is that children are, by their very nature, creatures of the 'now,' living fully immersed in each present moment. This month, pull out your dusty, old funny-bone, the one that used to keep you in stitches when you were a child, and laugh, on purpose, every day with your child. You'll be amazed at how a good belly laugh can turn even the worst day into something a little easier to handle and how much a giggle-fest can heal the little rifts that tend to occur in the parent/child connection throughout each day.

October (Step 10)

If you build it, they will come! ~ A shared project can offer a real chance to get to know your child on an entirely new level, so this month find something to build together. Choose something they are interested in, whether it's a model rocket or tree fort, and watch them blossom as they learn and build and grow. Your role is supportive--finding the materials, helping to read the instructions, offering suggestions or help when they struggle, etc. Simply being there through the process will enrich your connection with your child and offer you valuable insights into their interests and learning style, which will provide tools for you to use when helping them with their homework or if you are homeschooling them.

November (Step 11)

Gratitude is an attitude! ~ Teaching our children to be grateful involves far more than simply instructing them to say, *"Thank you."* We all want to be appreciated, and children are no different. Remember, modeling the things we want to see in our children is the single most powerful mode of instruction, so living a life of gratitude ourselves goes a long way toward raising our little ones to be happy, grateful humans. Openly appreciating our children, telling them what we like about them, and thanking them for the things they do is a sure-fire way of inspiring an attitude of gratitude in their little hearts. This month, be intentional in finding things to praise in your children. Don't be falsely enthusiastic or use *"Good job!"* as a brush-off to get them to leave you alone. Instead, honestly tell them what you like about them. Tell them *"Thank you"* when they remember to brush their teeth without being told or help their little sister with her block tower. Let them know you think their artwork is beautiful and don't hesitate to give them a pat on the back for a job well done when they straighten their room. Remember, it is the hungry child, not the satisfied child, who craves food, and, in the same way, it is *unmet* needs that lead to attention seeking behaviors and *unspoken* approval that can create 'praise junkies' as the unpraised child seeks to fill the very human need we all have for validation.

December (Step 12)

Celebrate! ~ Take time this month to give yourself a pat on the back for working toward your goal of becoming a gentle parent. Congratulate yourself for all that you've accomplished and take stock of your successes as well as your failures. Don't focus on your mistakes. Simply learn from them, forgive yourself, and move forward. Look back at where you were as a parent a year ago and compare that to where you are now. Don't worry if you haven't come as far as you'd like. Remember to give yourself grace. Life is for living and learning and growing, and another year is about to start with a chance to move forward into a new beginning. Everything you've invested in your children in the last year has been worthwhile, and everything you'll invest in the coming years will build on the foundation you've begun. So take this month to celebrate *you* and to enjoy the return on your investment!

~~~~~~~~

Do you see a theme throughout this gentle parenting '12-step program'? Getting to know and enjoy your children as individuals, intentionally focusing on building and maintaining a strong and healthy parent/child connection, and living what you want your children to learn are the bedrocks of gentle parenting. Walking through these steps, revisiting them when you find yourself struggling, and appreciating the incredible, miraculous gifts that each individual child brings into the world will keep you growing as a gentle parent day after day, month after month, year after year.

Live. Laugh. Love. Enjoy!

Appendix B

Backtalk is Communication...LISTEN

[From *Whispers Through Time: Communication Through the Ages and Stages of Childhood*]

With more than ninety-percent of parents admitting to spanking or otherwise physically punishing their children at least occasionally, mainstream American parenting can certainly be defined as punitive. If you go to the library or browse the shelves at Barnes & Noble or check out Amazon's best sellers in the parenting genre, you will find a predominance of popular, punishment-based, obedience-focused parenting guides. Whether its spanking or time outs or removal of privileges or time confined in their room, the vast majority of children in the United States are raised with punitive parenting.

When it comes to children talking back to parents, many of these punitive parenting guides dictate a zero-tolerance policy. By their definition, backtalk is often characterized as verbal or emotional abuse of parents, defiance, rudeness, or threats:

- Verbal or emotional abuse of parents is considered any statement that insults or hurts a parent such as, "You're so mean!" or "I wish I didn't even have parents!" or "I hate you!"

- Defiance is any statement containing the word "No" in response to a parental command.

- Rudeness is defined as anything from deep sighs to rolled eyes to stomped feet.

- Threats are any statements that give conditions such as, "If you take away my cell phone, I'll just go get a new one!" or "If you don't drive me to my friend's house, I'm walking there!"

These parenting guides direct parents to decide which punishment to mete out when their child talks back to them, specifying that the deciding factor should be whichever punishment would be the most unpleasant, painful, and distressing for the child. Punishments are to be carried out swiftly and without discussion. When the retribution for the child's actions is over, it is to be followed with a lecture laying down the laws of the family. Again, no discussion is allowed, but if the child expresses appropriate penitence, love and hugs can then be offered.

In addition to the sick feeling in the pit of my stomach at the thought of children being subjected to this kind of harsh, punitive parenting, I'm saddened by the upside-down reasoning that shuts communication down instead of utilizing it to bring healing, understanding, and restoration to the parent/child relationship.

Take a look at the order of parenting prescribed: First, punishment meted out by the parent. Second, lecture delivered by the parent. Third, conditional reconnection based on a proper expression of remorse to the parent from the child.

In gentle parenting, the order and intent of parenting would be the polar opposite: First would come listening for the need behind the behavior and reconnecting with the child at the point of need. Second, would be initiating a two-way communication about the problem and brainstorming about how to address the issue in ways that will meet everyone's needs. Third, would be offering guidance and equipping the child with better ways to express needs in the future.

The punitive parenting approach focuses on the child as the problem and attempts to solve the problem by 'fixing' the child through intentionally unpleasant external forces.

The gentle parenting approach focuses on the child having a problem and attempts to help the child solve the problem through connection, communication, and inviting cooperation.

Now look at the definitions of backtalk—verbal and emotional abuse of parents, defiance, rudeness, and threats. The questions that immediately arise are: What about the parents? Are they held to the same standards as the children? Or do they threaten? Do they say 'No'? Do they sigh? Do they hurt their children?

As parents, our actions will always be reflected in our children's behavior. Children learn what they live. No amount of lecturing can undo the powerful impact on a child of their parent's own behavior and choices.

When a child backtalks, sometimes also referred to as mouthing-off or sassing, they are in the throes of a huge, internal maelstrom of emotion. Whatever they are reacting to in the moment, whether it's being told 'no' about something or being asked to do or not do something, it is rarely those issues that are at the root of the problem. The moment at hand is just the tipping point causing a fissure in the child's heart that lets out a bit of the steam inside. The real concern should be that there is, metaphorically, steam in the child's heart to begin with.

It is at this point that parents have the opportunity to model self-control and self-regulation by controlling their own knee-jerk reaction to their child's backtalk. Instead of meeting fire with fire, childish outburst with childish parental outburst, child's tantrum with adult tantrum, parents can slow down, breathe through their own emotions, and then listen through the fiery storm of their child's words to the hurt, fear, and anger behind the words.

In the same way that "a gentle answer turns away wrath," a soft-voiced, "Let's take a minute and calm down so we can work through this together, okay?" from a parent is a magical, healing balm that immediately begins to diffuse tough situations and creates an atmosphere in which connection and communication can bring effective, peaceful solutions not only to the issue at hand, but also to the inner turmoil that prompted the outburst in the first place.

Meeting a child at their point of need when that need is expressed through meltdowns, yelling, disrespect, or defiance takes patience, self-control, and empathy on the part of a parent, which can be a huge growth experience for the parent if they, themselves, were not parented that way. But the impact of living those positive life skills in front of our children is immeasurable.

Parenting isn't a perfect science and parents aren't perfect people, but creating an overall atmosphere of respect in a home starts with the parents modeling respect in their own tone of voice, in their own reactions to stressful situations, in their own interactions with their children.

It's not easy, for sure. But the best things, the most valuable things, in life rarely are. Working toward being understanding, available, and responsive to our children's needs yields a priceless return in our relationship as the years fly by and adulthood looms. Not meeting those needs, though, may have serious negative consequences...

Dear Daughter,

You entered your teen years with a bang a few years ago, and the explosions have been shattering our home ever since. I've begged, threatened, bribed, and punished; cried, shouted, and bargained; but I just can't find a way to reach you anymore. You constantly say I don't listen to you, but how can I when you won't talk to me? You say I don't understand you, but how can I when you push me away? You say we aren't a family, but then spend every day with earphones in your ears, blocking us out. You ask me why I hate you, then roll your eyes when I tell you I love you. How did it come to this? We used to be such a happy family. Please, let me be there for you during this huge transition in your life. Let's really try to communicate with each other. I'm just lost here, honey, and I need you to reach out and help me reconnect with you. I love you.

Your Dad

'Dear' Dad,

Happy family? Are you kidding me? No, I guess not. You never did get it. Okay, you asked, so I'll tell you. You were always happy because you were always in control. Want to know why I don't talk to you now? Because you never listened when I was little. When I was scared in my room at night and called you, you either ignored me or threatened to spank me if I didn't go to sleep. I'd lay there, crying so hard I'd almost throw up, terrified of the sounds and shadows in my room, but even more terrified of you. So, sorry, but I don't buy that you're 'there for me' when it's only ever been at your own convenience. When you were mad at something I'd done and I tried to explain myself, you'd call it backtalk and smack me in the mouth. So forgive me if I don't really believe you when you say you want to 'communicate' with me now. When I'd try to show you a dance I'd made up or tell you about how someone had pushed me on the playground, you couldn't even be bothered to look away from your stupid computer while I was talking, so if I'm wrapped up in my electronics, I learned that little trick from you, Father Dear. Oh, and reconnect? Really? That implies that we were once connected. But when I was a little girl and invited you into my world and asked you to play with me, you were always too busy. So if you don't understand me, sorry, but that invitation expired years ago. Want to know why I think you hate me? Because your actions told me so. Your 'love' is just words.

'Your' Daughter

Not all children react this way to harsh, punitive, control-based parenting, of course. Some children, due to personality, other influences and mentors in their lives, or simply as a survival instinct, will turn out okay despite how they are parented.

But 'okay' is too mediocre a goal when it comes to growing our children into the adults who will one day lead our world. Instead of raising children who turn out okay despite their childhood, let's raise children who turn out extraordinary because of their childhood. Let's grow excellent, outstanding, remarkable adults who will be world changers for the next generation and the generations to come.

Appendix C

The Still, Small Voice

[From *Jesus, the Gentle Parent: Gentle Christian Parenting*]

"...a great and strong wind tore into the mountains and broke the rocks in pieces before the Lord, but the Lord was not in the wind; and after the wind an earthquake, but the Lord was not in the earthquake; and after the earthquake a fire, but the Lord was not in the fire; and after the fire a still small voice..."
1 Kings 19:11-12

When you read God's Word, what do you hear? Do you hear the voice of an angry, overbearing, condemning Father demanding instant and unquestioning obedience? Do you hear the voice of an intimidating, domineering, distant Father issuing threats and calling down curses on your head?

So often when we read God's Word we hear what we've heard from the pulpit instead of hearing the voice of a Father who loves unconditionally, sacrificially, and eternally. And so often what we've heard from the pulpit is accusation, damnation, and condemnation. It's no wonder we have problems trusting in God's unconditional love if all we hear are commands, demands, and reprimands echoed in those misguided voices.

I recently read a story about someone who asked God to move a mountain and was answered with a prompt, "Yes!" and a shovel.[42] (Esther, Girl at the End of the World) That's what it can feel like when you're digging and sifting and winnowing your way through years of hearing human interpretations of God's Word spoken from the pulpit and from Sunday school teachers and Bible camp counselors and parents and friends and relatives, etc.

Working our way through all of the human ideas about what God says and who God is and what he wants and how he relates to us to a place where we find God's heart and can actually hear God's voice ourselves and get to know him personally and feel him moving and guiding and loving us is a hugely challenging, intensely moving, constantly evolving, and incredibly enlightening journey.

Humans aren't perfect and, no matter how wise, how conscientious, how educated they are, the simple fact is that the human mind cannot fully grasp the mind and heart of God and, therefore, their interpretations of the Bible must always be regarded with careful examination instead of absolute faith.

The thing is, though, that we *can* find God's heart. We have direct access. God's heart came to earth as a baby, lived and loved and laughed with God's precious children, and then was hung on a Cross, died, and was resurrected, defeating death for God's children once and for all.

But after years and years of hearing humans tell us what God said and what he meant in his Word, it can be incredibly hard to discern God's voice for ourselves. Let's take a look at some verses and listen carefully for the "the still, small voice" that whispers from the heart of love...

> *"Do not be anxious about anything, but in every situation, by prayer and petition, with thanksgiving, present your requests to God. And the peace of God, which transcends all understanding, will guard your hearts and your minds in Christ Jesus." (Philippians 4:6-7)*

Listen for the still, small voice...comforting, not controlling:

> *"Don't worry, little one. I'm right here. Come to me with what you need. I'll help."*

Can you hear the voice of comfort?

"'Love the Lord your God with all your heart and with all your soul and with all your strength and with all your mind' and, 'Love your neighbor as yourself'... "Do this and you will live." (Luke 10:27 & 28)

Listen for the still, small voice...tender, not tyrannical:

"Love me as I have loved you, wholeheartedly, extravagantly, with everything you have and everything you are, and love my children the same way, fully accepting, graciously giving, because that is where you will find me and, in me, you will find life."

Can you hear the voice of tenderness?

> *"Be still, and know that I am God."* (Psalm 46:10)

> Listen for the still, small voice...reassuring, not reprimanding:

> *"I've got this, so you can relax and trust me, little one."*

> Can you hear the voice of reassurance?

"Be dressed in readiness, and keep your lamps lit." (Luke 12:35)

Listen for the still, small voice...wise, not wrathful:

"Don't worry, little ones, put on the safe covering of Jesus and keep your love and your hope alive."

Can you hear the voice of wisdom?

> *"The Lord's bond-servant must not be quarrelsome, but be kind to all, able to teach, patient when wronged."* (2 Timothy 2:24)

> Listen for the still, small voice...counseling, not commanding:

"You're attached to me at the heart, my children, so let your heart reflect my peace, my kindness, my teaching, my forgiveness."

Can you hear the voice of counsel?

As travelers looked to the stars in ancient times to guide them on their journeys, so we look to God as our guiding light. The Hebrew word *halal* means to 'look toward another as a shining light,'[1,2,3] so when the psalmist says, '*Praise Yah (halelu-Yah)*' it literally means to "Look to Yah (the Lord) as the light that will guide you on your journey."

And so listen, parents, for the still, small voice of love, wisdom, and guidance from God, the *only* source of truth. The viewpoints, analysis, and interpretations of scripture that you've read here in *Jesus, the Gentle Parent*, like all others, must be examined, discussed, and prayed over instead of taken on faith. Keep your faith for God alone. When you read the words in this book, don't accept them. Question them. Challenge them. Test them. Pray about them. Ask God to give you eyes to see and ears to hear so that you can make your own decisions based on God's wise and wonderful counsel.

"But blessed are your eyes, because they see; and your ears, because they hear. For truly I say to you that many prophets and righteous men desired to see what you see, and did not see it, and to hear what you hear, and did not hear it."
Matthew 13:16-17

Reader reviews of the Little Hearts Handbook series by
L.R.Knost:

*Two Thousand Kisses a Day: Gentle Parenting Through the
Ages and Stages*

Calm, Reassuring, Likable ~ Written in L.R.Knost's signature
easy-to-read and conversational style, *Two Thousand Kisses a
Day* offers an overview of gentle parenting from birth through
young adulthood along with concrete suggestions and insights
into how to implement gentle parenting in each stage of
childhood. Her seasoned and practical approach based on
extensive child development research and years of parent
mentoring as well as over twenty-five years of parenting her six
children is as likable as it is reassuring. Parents with children of
any age will find this information-packed book with its bite-
sized chapters and practical approach to parenting a helpful and
encouraging addition to their home library, as well as a welcome
gift for new or struggling parents.

*Whispers Through Time: Communication Through the Ages and
Stages of Childhood*

Sweet, Funny, Insightful ~ Award-winning *Whispers Through
Time* by L.R. Knost is destined to be a dog-eared favorite,
passed down from generation to generation. L.R. Knost shows
parents how to find their own answers for their own children and
their own families in this guidebook that challenges
conventional thinking with a wisdom born of experience and a
healthy dose of research to back it up. Written with the same
unique blend of sweetness and humor, grit and honesty,
reassurance and insight that made L.R. Knost's first book, *Two
Thousand Kisses a Day: Gentle Parenting Through the Ages and
Stages*, a best-seller, *Whispers Through Time* has become a
runaway hit in its own right.

The Gentle Parent: Positive, Practical, Effective Discipline

Relaxed, Reassuring, Practical ~ Written by L.R.Knost, best-selling, award-winning author of *Two Thousand Kisses a Day* and *Whispers Through Time*, *The Gentle Parent: Positive, Practical, Effective Discipline* shares the simple secrets of a peaceful, happy home in the Three C's of gentle discipline—Connection, Communication, and Cooperation. In her signature relaxed and poetic style, L.R.Knost gently guides parents through the steps of applying the Three C's in real-life scenarios from tantrums to defiance to parenting a strong-willed child to healing a broken parent/child relationship. Practical and proven, this newest installment in the Little Hearts Handbook parenting series will be tucked into diaper bags, kept handy on nightstands, and shared with good friends for its research-backed, experience-based, and humor-rich insights, ideas, and inspiration.

Jesus, the Gentle Parent: Gentle Christian Parenting

Intelligent, Well-Researched, Compassionate ~ L.R.Knost has done it again. With her compassionate tone, relational style, and intelligent, well-researched writing, *Jesus, the Gentle Parent: Gentle Christian Parenting* Jesus, the Gentle Parent is like a refreshing, peaceful walk through the scriptures with a friendly and knowledgeable tour guide. This book differs from *Two Thousand Kisses a Day*, *Whispers Through Time*, and *The Gentle Parent: Positive, Practical, Effective Discipline* in that it takes a Christian approach to parenting as L.R. takes on big names in the Christian child-training sect such as Dr. James Dobson, Tedd Tripp, Gary Ezzo, and Michael Pearl, breaking down their doctrine and reexamining such issues as spanking, instant obedience, submission, free will, and more in light of the original Hebrew and Greek texts of the scriptures. As always, L.R. offers gentle parenting alternatives along with real-life examples of their applications, but in *Jesus, the Gentle Parent: Gentle Christian Parenting* she goes even further and shares parenting insights based on the life of Jesus that will turn the mainstream Christian world on its head. This is truly a grace-based parenting book which shows parents how to be "their children's first taste of God" by following in the gentle, wise, grace-filled footsteps of Jesus.

References:

1. Schore, A.N. (2000). Attachment and the regulation of the right brain. Attachment & Human Development, 2, 23-47.

2. Sears, Dr. William. SIDS: A Parent's Guide to Understanding and Preventing Sudden Infant Death Syndrome . Little Brown & Co, 1995. Print. <http://www.amazon.com/SIDS-Parents-Understanding-Preventing-Syndrome/dp/0316779121/ref=sr_1_1?s=books&ie=UTF8&qid=1360194660&sr=1-1&keywords=0316779121>.

3. Melissa Bartick, MD, MSca, Arnold Reinhold, MBA, . "The Burden of Suboptimal Breastfeeding in the United States: A Pediatric Cost Analysis." Journal of the American Academy of Pediatrics . (2010): n. page. Web. 6 Feb. 2013. <http://pediatrics.aappublications.org/content/early/2010/0 4/05/peds.2009-1616.abstract>.

4. World Health Organization. <http://www.who.int/topics/breastfeeding/>.

5. Sears, Dr. William. Feeding the Picky Eater: 17 Tips. <http://www.askdrsears.com/topics/feeding-infants-toddlers/feeding-picky-eater-17-tips>.

6. Healy, Melissa. "The Mind Unchecked." Los Angeles Times 01 12 2009, Health n. pag. Web. 9 Oct. 2013. <http://latimesblogs.latimes.com/booster_shots/2009/12/th e-mind-unchecked-is-babys-lack-of-selfcontrol-key-to-early-learning.html>.

7. Disney Studios. Finding Nemo. 2003

8. Park, Alice. "The Long-Term Effects of Spanking." Time Magazine. 03 05 2010: n. page. Print. <http://content.time.com/time/magazine/article/0,9171,19 83895,00.html>.

9. Canadian Medical Association Journal. "Physical punishment of children potentially harmful to their long-term development." ScienceDaily, 6 Feb. 2012. Web. 9 Oct. 2013.

10. Corporal Punishment. <http://en.wikipedia.org/wiki/Corporal_punishment>.

11. Scientific American. <http://www.scientificamerican.com/blog/post.cfm?id=sh ould-parents-spank-their-kids-pro-2009-08-07>

12. The Butterfly Effect.
     <http://en.wikipedia.org/wiki/The_Butterfly_Effect

13. HuffPost Parents.
     <http://www.huffingtonpost.com/2012/04/17/police-
     handcuff-ga-kinder_n_1430749.html

31753791R00080